A KEY TO THE NEW LITURGICAL CONSTITUTION

The New

A KEY TO
Liturgical Constitution

An Alphabetical Analysis
by Angelus A. De Marco, O.F.M.

Desclee Company
New York - Tournai - Paris - Rome

1964

The English text of the Constitution on the Sacred Liturgy is based on that released by the United States Bishops' Press Panel.

IMPRIMI POTEST
  Rev. Harold Blake, O.F.M.
  May 29, 1964

NIHIL OBSTAT
  Very Rev. Walter J. Schmitz, S.S.
  Censor Deputatus

IMPRIMATUR
  ✠ Patrick A. O'Boyle
  Archbishop of Washington

June 30, 1964

The nihil obstat and imprimatur are official declarations that a book or pamphlet is free of doctrinal or moral error. No implication is contained therein that those who have granted the nihil obstat and the imprimatur agree with the contents, opinions or statements expressed.

Preface

Pope John XXIII, in announcing his intention of calling an ecumenical Council, expressed the sincere wish that it would be a new "Pentecost"—a renewal in the life of the Church. The primary objective of the Supreme Pontiff immediately struck a responsive chord in the hearts of Christians throughout the world and seemed to have answered their most ardent desires.

On December 4, 1963, the first step in this plan of renewal was made by the promulgation of the Constitution on the Liturgy by Pope Paul VI at the close of the second session of the Council. Thus, the true place of liturgical reform within the framework of the Church's inner renewal was clearly established.

> This sacred Council has several aims in view: it desires to impart an ever increasing vigor to the Christian life of the faithful; to adapt more suitably to the needs of our own times those institutions which are subject to change; to foster whatever can promote union among all who believe in Christ; to strengthen whatever can help to call the whole of mankind into the household of the Church. The Council, therefore, sees particularly cogent reasons for undertaking the reform and promotion of the liturgy.

A decisive appraisal of the inestimable value of the Liturgy and consequently its pastoral importance for building the Christian community and invigorating the heart of Christian living through restoration and reform should come as no sudden surprise. The Liturgical Movement and its program of reform has a long history. Time and again the Supreme Pontiffs have endeavored to direct its cause: Gregory the Great, Gregory VII, Innocent III, Pius V; and in our own century, Pius X, and Pius XI, and above all, Pius XII, through whose indomitable efforts the indifference and misunderstanding, which threatened to stifle its development, was universally overcome. His three Encyclicals: *Divino Afflante Spiritu*, *Mystici Corporis*, and *Mediator Dei*, without doubt, not only marked the turning point in the spiritual life of the Church, but also laid the solid foundation for all liturgical progress of the future.

From then on reforms were enacted. The Liturgy and its development, it relation to Theology, its pastoral character and efficacy became the object of numerous studies. Enthusiasm began to spread based on the conviction that the Liturgy is wholly and intrinsically pastoral. Liturgical gatherings of small groups met to discuss the urgent needs, problems, and difficulties of liturgical renewal. In 1956, at the conclusion of the International Congress on Pastoral Liturgy which was held at Assisi-Rome, it became obvious for the first time what direction the Movement had finally taken. No longer was it the interest and concern of a few, but now it was the concern of the whole Church in which Pius XII could see it as "a sign of the providential dispositions of God for our time, of the presence of the Holy Spirit in the Church."

During the Pontificate of John XXIII it began to be accepted more than ever before that the Movement is a pastoral factor of primary importance, that the Liturgy in itself is wholly pastoral and demands by its nature a public and shared expression.

Pope Paul VI in ascending the throne of Peter pledged the efforts of his Pontificate to the work of John. Keenly aware of the central position which the Sacred Liturgy occupies in the life of the Church—its spiritual and pastoral potentialities—he immediately put all the resources of his energy at the service of a cause which could reap for all mankind, union and peace. Nothing was more urgent in this moment of the Church's history than a renewed realization that the Church has only one objective: to bring men to share in the divine life that has been made available to them through Jesus Christ. For this reason, in promulgating the Constitution the Pontiff described it as,

> the first subject to be examined and also the first, in a certain sense, because of its intrinsic value in the life of the Church.

Thus, Vatican Council II has given to posterity a document unparalleled in the history of the Church; a criterion with inexhaustible capacities for rediscovering Christ! May the study of this Constitution be a means of giving all the faithful a better understanding and love for the Liturgy as the primary and indispensable source from which they derive the true Christian spirit!

Angelus A. De Marco, O.F.M.
Holy Name College
Washington, D.C.

A KEY TO THE NEW LITURGICAL CONSTITUTION

Abbot, CONCELEBRATION AT MASS FOR BLESSING OF, is
permitted: *Facultatem concelebrandi ad Missam in Benedictione Abbatis Concilio extendere placuit (57:1.1.c)*.

ACCLAMATIONS, BY MEANS OF, the faithful are able to
actively participate in the liturgy: *Ad actuosam participationem promovendam, populi acclamationes foveantur
(30)*.

ACOLYTES, exercise a genuine liturgical function: *ministrantes vero ministerio liturgico funguntur (29)*.

    THE OFFICE OF, to be discharged with sincere piety and
decorum: *munus suum tali sincera pietate et ordine
exerceant (29)*.

    TO BE IMBUED WITH THE SPIRIT OF THE LITURGY: *oportet
eos spiritu Liturgiae (29)*.

    TO BE TRAINED, to perform their functions in a correct
and orderly manner: *ad partes suas rite et ordinate
obeundas institui (29)*.

ACTIONS AND GESTURES, BY MEANS OF, the faithful
are able to actively participate in the liturgy: *Ad actuosam participationem promovendam, populi actiones seu
gestus foveantur (30)*.

ACTIVE PARTICIPATION IN THE LITURGY. See PARTICIPATION.

ADAPTATION, LITURGICAL, CUSTOMS AND DISCIPLINE
OF THE SACRED SEASONS, to be reviewed in accordance
with the provisions of Art. 39 and 40, if considered necessary on account of local conditions: *Annus liturgicus
. . . consuetudinibus et disciplinis iuxta nostra aetatis
condiciones . . . accommodationes secundum locorum
condiciones, si quae forte necessariae sint, fiant ad
normam art. 39 et 40 (107)*.

    EXPERIMENTS, to be made over a period of time suited
for this purpose, with the permission of the National
Conference of Bishops: *Ut autem aptatio cum neces-*

saria circumspectione fiat, eidem auctoritati ecclesiasticae territoriali ab Apostolica Sede facultas tribuetur, *si casus ferat, ut in quibusdam coetibus ad id aptis
et per determinatum tempus necessaria praevia experimenta permittat et dirigat (40.2).*

LENTEN PRACTICES, should be fostered in ways that are
possible in our own times and in different regions, and
according to the circumstances of the faithful: *Praxis
paenitentialis, iuxta nostrae aetatis et diversarum regionum possibilitates necnon fidelium condiciones,
foveatur (110).*

LITURGICAL BOOKS, provisions to be made according to
different groups, regions, and peoples, especially in
mission lands, provided that the substantial unity of
the Roman rite is preserved: *Servata substantiali unitate ritus romani, legitimis varietatibus et aptationibus
ad diversos coetus, regiones, populos, praesertim in
Missionibus, locus relinquatur, etiam cum libri liturgici
recognoscuntur (38).*

MATINS, to be arranged so that it may be recited at any
hour of the day: *ita accommodetur ut qualibet diei
hora recitari possit (89.c).*

MISSION INITIATION RITES IN RITUAL, may be admitted
along with those already found in Christian tradition,
according to the norm laid down in Art. 37–40 of this
Constitution: *In terris Missionum, praeter ea quae
in traditione christiana habentur, illa etiam elementa
initiationis admitti liceat, quae apud unumquemque
populum in usu esse reperiuntur, quatenus ritui christiano accommodari possunt, ad normam art. 37–40
huius Constitutionis (65).*

MISSION MUSICAL TRADITIONS, are to be admitted since
they play a great part in the religious and social life
of the natives: *Cum in regionibus quibusdam, Missionum, gentes inveniantur quibus propria est traditio
musica, magnum momentum in earum vita religiosa
ac sociali habens, huic musicae aestimatio debita*

necnon locus congruus praebeatur . . . quam in cultu
ad earum indolem accommodando, ad mentem art.
39 et 40 (119).

NATIONAL CONFERENCE OF BISHOPS, to carefully and pru-
dently consider which elements from the traditions
and culture of individual peoples might appropriately
be admitted into divine worship. Those that are judged
useful or necessary should then be submitted to the
Apostolic See, by whose consent they may be introduced: *A competenti auctoritate territoriali, de qua
in art. 22:2, sedulo et prudenter consideretur quid,
hoc in negotio, ex traditionibus ingenioque singulorum
populorum opportune in cultum divinum admitti
possit. Aptationes quae utiles vel necessariae existimantur, Apostolicae Sedi proponantur, de ipsius consensu introducendae (40.1).*

NATIVE CUSTOMS OF VARIOUS RACES AND PEOPLES, are re-
spected and fostered by the Church. Anything in these
which is not indissolubly bound up with superstition
and error . . . she admits, so long as they harmonize
with the true and authentic spirit of the liturgy:
*Ecclesia, in iis quae fidem aut bonum totius com-
munitatis non tangunt, rigidam unius tenoris formam
ne in Liturgia quidem imponere cupit; quinimmo,
variarum gentium populorumque animi ornamenta ac
dotes colit et provehit; quidquid vero in populorum
moribus indissolubili vinculo superstitionibus erroribusque non adstipulatur, benevole perpendit ac, si
potest, sartum tectumque servat, immo quandoque in
ipsam Liturgiam admittit, dummodo cum rationibus
veri et authentici spiritus liturgici congruat (37).*

REGIONAL DIFFERENCES IN RITUALS, are admitted. They
are to be reviewed by the Apostolic See and then introduced into the regions for which they have been
prepared: *Iuxta novam Ritualis romani editionem,
Ritualis particularia, singularum regionum necessita-*

tibus, etiam quoad linguam, accommodata. . . . ab
Apostolica Sede recognitis, in regionibus ad quas pertinet adhibeantur (63.b).

RITE OF BURIAL OF DEAD, should correspond more closely
to the circumstances and traditions found in various
regions: *Ritus exsequiarum . . . condicionibus et
traditionibus singularum regionum . . . melius respondeat (81).*

SACRED FURNISHINGS AND VESTMENTS, MATERIALS AND
FORMS OF, are to be admitted according to the needs
and customs of their different regions: *quoad materiam et formam sacrae supellectilis et indumentorum,
territorialibus Episcoporum Coetibus facultas tribuitur res aptandi necessitatibus et moribus locorum, ad
normam art. 22 huius Constitutionis (128).*

STYLES OF ART, are admitted from every period according
to the natural talents and circumstances of the peoples,
and the needs of the various rites: *Ecclesia nullum
artis stilum veluti proprium habuit, sed secumdum
gentium indoles ac condiciones atque variorum Rituum necessitates modos cuiusvis aetatis admisit (123).*

STYLES OF MUSIC, all forms of true art, having the necessary qualities, the Church approves and admits into
divine worship: *Ecclesia autem omnes verae artis
formas, debitis praeditas dotibus probat easque in
cultum divinum admittit (112).*

TREASURES OF THE ROMAN OFFICE, to be so arranged
that all those to whom they are handed on may more
extensively and easily draw profit from them: *In instauratione vero peragenda, venerabilis ille romani
Officii saecularis thesaurus ita aptetur, ut latius et
facilius eo frui possint omnes quibus traditur (90).*

ADDITIONS IN LITURGY, are forbidden by any unauthorized person: *Quapropter nemo omnino alius,
etiamsi sit sacerdos, quidquam proprio marte in Liturgia
addat, demat, aut mutet (22:3).*

ADOPTION AS GOD'S CHILDREN, by Baptism: *Sic per Baptismum homines . . . spiritum accipiunt adoptionis filiorum, "in quo clamamus: Abba, Pater"* (Rom. 8:15) (6).

ADULT BAPTISM. See BAPTISM, ADULT.

ADULT CATECHUMENATE, TO BE RESTORED, and used at the discretion of the local ordinary: *Instauretur catechumenatus adultorum pluribus gradibus distinctus, de iudicio Ordinarii loci in usum deducendus* (64).

ADVENT, BIBLE SERVICES IN, to be encouraged: *Foveatur sacra Verbi Dei celebratio . . . in aliquibus feriis Adventus* (35.4).

at functions without a priest, they are particularly to be commended: *maxime in locis quas sacerdote carent* (35.4).

ALTARS, LAWS FOR CONSTRUCTION OF, to be revised: *Canones et statuta ecclesiastica, quae rerum externarum ad sacrum cultum pertinentium spectant, praesertim . . . altarium formam et aedificationem* (128).

ANCIENT RITES, the Church regards them all worthy of equal veneration: *Traditioni denique fideliter obsequens, Sacrosanctum Concilium declarat Sanctam Matrem Ecclesiam omnes ritus legitime agnitos aequo iure atque honore habere* (4).

ANOINTING OF THE SICK, NUMBER OF, to be adapted to the occasion: *Unctionum numerum pro opportunitate accommodetur* (75).

PRAYERS, to be revised, so as to correspond to the varying conditions of the sick who receive the sacrament: *orationes ad ritum Unctionis infirmorum pertinentes ita recognoscantur, ut respondeant variis condicionibus infirmorum, qui Sacramentum suscipiunt* (75).

TIME OF ADMINISTRATION, as soon as any one of the faithful begins to be in danger of death from sickness or old age: *Tempus opportunum eam recipiendi iam* certe habetur cum fidelis incipit esse in periculo mortis propter infirmitatem vel senium *(73).*

VIATICUM AND, continuous rite to be prepared according to which the sick man is anointed after he has made his confession and before he receives viaticum: *Conficiatur Ordo continuus secundum quem Unctio aegroto conferatur post confessionem et ante receptionem Viatici (74).*

ANTIPHONS, BY RECITING, the faithful are able to actively participate in the liturgy: *Ad actuosam participationem promovendam, populi . . . antiphonae foveantur (30).*

APOSTLES, MISSION OF, to preach the gospel to every creature, and to accomplish the work of salvation by means of sacrifice and sacraments: *Ideoque, sicut Christus missus est a Patre, ita et ipse Apostolos. . . . misit, non solum ut, predicantes Evangelium omni creaturae . . . sed etiam ut, quod annuntiabant, opus salutis per Sacrificium et Sacramenta (6).*

APOSTOLATE, LITURGICAL, to restore and promote the full and active participation by all the people: *Quae totius populi plena et actuosa participatio, in instauranda et fovenda sacra Liturgia, summopere est attendenda (14).*

OF PASTORS, to ensure that the faithful take part in the liturgy fully aware of what they are doing, actively engaged in the rite, and enriched by its effects: *sacris pastoribus advigilandam est ut in actione liturgica . . . fideles scienter, actuose et fructuose eandem participent (11).*

OF PRIESTS, to understand ever more fully what it is that they are doing when they perform the sacred rites, and to live the liturgical life and share it with the faithful entrusted to their care: *Sacerdotes, in vinea Domini iam operantes, omnibus mediis opportunis iuventur ut plenius semper quae in functionibus sacris agunt in-*

*tellegant, vitam liturgicam vivant, eamque cum fideli-
bus sibi commissis communicent (18).*

APOSTOLIC SEE, SUPREME AUTHORITY OF.

TO CONFIRM ADAPTATIONS, which are judged useful or
necessary by the competent territorial ecclesiastical
authority mentioned in Art. 22:2. *A competenti auctoritate ecclesiastica territoriali, de qua in art. 22:2
. . . aptationes quae utiles vel necessariae existimantur, Apostolicae Sedi proponantur, de ipsius consensu
introducendae (40.1).*

TO CONFIRM DECREES OF NATIONAL CONFERENCES OF
BISHOPS REGARDING USE OF VERNACULAR, it is for the
competent territorial ecclesiastical authority mentioned
in Art. 22:2 to decide whether, and to what extent,
the vernacular language is to be used; their decrees are
to be approved, that is, confirmed by the Apostolic See:
*est competentis auctoritatis ecclesiasticae territorialis,
de qua in art. 22:2 . . . de usu et modo linguae vernaculae statuere, actis ab Apostolica Sede probatis seu
confirmatis (36:3).*

TO DETERMINE CASES WHEN COMMUNION UNDER BOTH
KINDS MAY BE GRANTED, as for instance, to the newly ordained in the Mass of their ordination, to the newly
professed in the Mass of their religious profession, and
to the newly baptized in the Mass which follows their
baptism: *Communio sub utraque specie . . . in casibus ab Apostolica Sede definiendis, tum clericis et
religiosis, tum laicis concedi potest, de iudicio Episcoporum, veluti ordinatis in Missa sacrae suae ordinationis, professis in Missa religiosae suae professionis,
neophytis in Missa quae Baptismum subsequitur (55).*

TO GRANT THE FACULTY OF EXPERIMENTING WITH ADAP-
TATIONS, to the territorial ecclesiastical authority:
*aptatio . . . eidem auctoritati ecclesiasticae territoriali
ab Apostolica Sede facultas tribuetur (40.2).*

TO REGULATE WORSHIP, this depends solely on the authority of the Church, that is, on the Apostolic See and, as laws may determine, on the bishop: *Sacrae liturgiae moderatio ab Ecclesiae auctoritate unice pendet: quae quidem est apud Apostolicam Sedem et, ad normam iuris, apud Episcopum (22:1)*.

TO REVIEW PARTICULAR RITUALS, which are adapted according to the needs of the different regions by the competent territorial ecclesiastical authority: *Ritualia particularia, singularum regionum necessitatibus . . . accommodata, a competenti ecclesiastica auctoritate territoriali de qua in art. 22:2 huius Constitutionis . . . actis ab Apostolica Sede recognitis (63.b)*.

APPROVAL, LITURGICAL. See APOSTOLIC SEE; BISHOPS; BISHOPS, NATIONAL CONFERENCE OF; ORDINARIES; ORDINARIES, LOCAL.

ARCHITECTURE, LAWS ON, that refer especially to the worthy and well planned construction of sacred buildings shall be revised: *Canones et statuta ecclesiastica, quae rerum externarum ad sacrum pertinentium apparatum spectant, praesertim quoad aedium sacrarum dignam et aptam constructionem (128)*.

ART, ALL STYLES OF, are admitted by the Church. She has adopted them from every period according to the natural talents and circumstances of peoples, and the needs of the various rites: *Ecclesia nullum artis stilum veluti proprium habuit, sed secundum gentium indoles ac condiciones atque variorum Rituum necessitates modos cuiusvis aetatis admisit (123)*.

BISHOPS TO WATCH OVER, they are to remove anything that is offensive to the true religious sense: *Curent Episcopi ut artificum opera, quae fidei et moribus, ac christianae pietati repugnent, offendantque sensum vere religiosum (124)*.

COMMISSION OF, shall be established in every diocese as far as possible: *in quavis dioecesi constituantur, quan-*

tum fieri potest, etiam Commissiones de Musica sacra et de Arte sacra (46).

CONTEMPORARY, approved by the Church, provided it adorns the sacred buildings and holy rites with due reverence and honor: Nostrorum etiam temporum atque omnium gentium et regionum arts liberum in Ecclesia exercitium habeat, dummodo sacris aedibus sacrisque ritibus debita reverentia debitoque honore inserviat (123).

FUNCTION IN WORSHIP, by their very nature the fine arts are oriented towards the infinite beauty of God; they achieve their purpose of redounding to God's praise and glory: Quae natura sua ad infinitam pulchritudinem divinam spectant . . . et Deo eiusdemque laudi et gloriae provehendae . . . (122).

ORDINARIES OF PLACE TO JUDGE, after hearing the diocesan commission on art, and if necessary, also other experts: In diiudicandis artis operibus Ordinarii locorum audiant Commissionem dioecesanam de Arte sacra, et, si casus ferat, alios viros valde peritos . . . (126).

ORDINARIES TO EXERCISE GOOD TASTE, rather than encourage sumptuous display: Curent Ordinarii ut artem vere sacram promoventes eique faventes potius nobilem intendant pulchritudinem quam meram sumptuositatem (124).

SCHOOLS OF, to be established so that artists may be trained: commendatur ut scholae vel Academiae de Arte Sacra ad artifices formandos instituantur in illis regionibus in quibus id visum fuerit (127).

ARTISTS, BISHOPS TO FOSTER, so as to imbue them with the spirit of sacred art and of the sacred liturgy: Episcopi vel per se ipsos vel per sacerdotes idoneos qui peritia et artis amore praediti sunt, artificum curam habeant, ut eos spiritu Artis sacrae et sacrae Liturgiae imbuant (127).

CHURCH HAS RIGHT TO JUDGE WORKS OF, deciding if they are in accordance with faith, piety, and the laws of tradition, and thereby suited for sacred use: *earum veluti arbitram Ecclesia iure semper se habuit, diiudicans inter artificum opera quae fidei, pietati legibusque religiose traditis congruerent, atque ad usum sacrum idonea haberentur (122).*

TO BE GUIDED BY RELIGION, to serve God's glory in holy Church: *artifices autem omnes, qui ingenio suo ducti, gloriae Dei in Ecclesia sancta servire intendunt . . . (127).*

ATTITUDES, BODILY, BY MEANS OF, the faithful are able to actively participate in the liturgy: *Ad actuosam participationem promovendam populi . . . corporis habitus foveantur (30).*

AUTHORITY, LITURGICAL, regulation of the sacred liturgy depends solely on the authority of the Church, that is, on the Apostolic See and, as laws may determine, on the bishop: *Sacrae Liturgiae moderatio ab Ecclesiae auctoritate unice pendet: quae quidem est apud Apostolicam Sedem et, ad normam iuris, apud Episcopum (22:1).* See also: BISHOPS, NATIONAL CONFERENCE OF.

BAPTISM, ADULT, RITES OF, are to be revised: not only the simpler rite, but also the more solemn one which must take into account the restored catechumenate: *Uterque ritus baptizandis adultos tum simplicior, tum, ratione habita catechumenatus instaurati, solemnior, recognoscatur (66).*

CONVERTS, RITE OF, to be revised for those validly baptized: the new form should indicate that they are now admitted to communion with the Church: *novus ritus conficiatur pro valide iam baptizatis, ad sacra catholica conversis, quo significetur eos in Ecclesiae communionem admitti (69).*

EFFECTS OF, men are plunged into the paschal mystery of Christ: they die with Him, are buried with Him, and

rise with Him; they receive the spirit of adoption as
sons "in which we cry: Abba, Father" (Rom. 8:15):
*Sic per Baptismum homines paschali Christi mysterio
inseruntur: commortui, consepulti, conresuscitati;
spiritum accipiunt adoptionis filiorum, "in quo clamamus Abba, Pater" (Rom. 8:15) (6).*

INFANTS, "ORDER OF SUPPLYING WHAT WAS OMITTED," to
be revised. This should manifest more fittingly and
clearly that the infant, baptized by the short rite, has
already been received into the Church: *Loco ritus qui
"Ordo supplendi omissa super infantem baptizatum"
appellatur, novus conficiatur quo apertius et congru-
entius indicetur infantem, qui ritu brevi baptizatus
fuerit, iam receptum esse in Ecclesiam (69).*

INFANTS, RITE OF, to be revised, and adapted to the cir-
cumstance that those to be baptized are, in fact, infants:
*Ritus baptizandi parvulos recognoscatur et verae in-
fantium condicioni accommodetur (67).*

> the role of parents and god-parents, and also their
> duties, should be brought out more clearly in the
> rite itself: *partem etiam parentum et patrinorum
> eorumque officia, in ipso ritu, magis pateant (67).*

> a shorter rite is to be drawn up, especially in mission
> lands, to be used by catechists, but also by the faith-
> ful in general when there is danger of death, and
> neither priest nor deacon is available: *Conficiator
> item Ordo brevior quo, praesertim in terris Mis-
> sionum, catechistae, et generatim, in periculo mortis,
> fideles, absente sacerdote vel diacone, uti possint
> (68).*

MASS FOR CONFERRING, shall be drawn up and inserted in
the Roman Missal: *Missali romano Missa propria "In
collatione Baptismi" inseratur (66).*

MISSION LANDS' INITIATION RITES OF, shall be admitted
into the Christian ritual along with those already found,
if possible: *In terris Missionum, praeter ea quae in
traditione christiana habentur, illa etiam elementa in-*

itiationis admitti liceat . . . quatenus ritui christiano accommodari possunt (65).

SHORTER RITE OF, shall be drawn up, especially for Mission lands, to be used by catechists and also by the faithful in general when there is danger of death and neither priest nor deacon is available: *Conficiatur item Ordo brevior quo, praesertim in terris Missionum, catechistae, et generatim, in periculo mortis, fideles, absente sacerdote vel diacono, uti possint (68).*

VARIANTS IN RITE OF, to be admitted and used at the discretion of the local ordinary, for occasions when a very large number are to be baptized together: *In ritu Baptismi ne desint accommodationes, de iudicio Ordinarii loci adhibendae, pro magno baptizandorum concursu (68).*

WATER OF, may be blessed within the rite itself by an approved shorter formula, except during Eastertide: *Aqua baptismalis, extra tempus paschale, in ipso ritu Baptismi probata formula breviore benedici potest (70).*

BAPTISMAL PROMISES, to be renewed before candidate receives Confirmation: *renovatio promissionum Baptismi convenienter ipsam Sacramenti Confirmationis susceptionem praecedet (71)*

BAPTISTERIES, LAWS ON, shall be revised: *Canones et statuta ecclesiastica, quae rerum externarum ad sacrum cultum pertinentium apparatum spectant, praesertim . . . baptisterii convenientiam et honorem (128).*

BAPTIZED, THE RIGHT AND DUTY OF, to participate in the liturgy: *Valde cupit Mater Ecclesia ut fideles universi ad plenam illam, consciam atque actuosam liturgicarum celebrationum participationem ducantur . . . ad quam populus christianus . . . vi Baptismatis ius habet et officium (14).*

BIBLE. See SCRIPTURE.

BIBLE SERVICES, TO BE ENCOURAGED, especially on the vigils of the more solemn feasts, on some weekdays in

Advent and Lent, and on Sundays and feast days: *Foveatur sacra Verbi Dei celebratio in solemniorum festorum pervigiliis, in aliquibus feriis Adventus et Quadragesimae, atque in dominicis et diebus festis (35.4).*

DEACON OR AUTHORIZED PERSON TO PRESIDE, in services without a priest: *in locis quae sacerdote carent: quo in casu celebrationem diaconus vel alius ab Episcopo delegatus dirigat (35.4).*

IN PLACES WITHOUT A PRIEST, are particularly recommended: *maxime in locis quae sacerdote carent (35.4).*

BISHOP, ALLOCUTION IN CONSECRATION OF, may be in the vernacular: *Allocutio Episcopi, initio Consecrationis, fieri potest lingua vernacula (76).*

AS HIGH PRIEST, from whom the life in Christ of his faithful is in some way derived and dependent: *Episcopus ut sacerdos magnus sui gregis habendus est, a quo vita suorum fidelium in Christo quodammodo derivatur et pendet (41).*

CLERGY AND FAITHFUL TO BE UNITED WITH, in the liturgical life of the parish, both theoretically and practically: *vita liturgica paroeciae eiusque relatio ad Episcopum in mente et praxi fidelium et cleri fovenda est (42).*

CONSECRATION CEREMONY OF, imposition of hands may be done by all bishops present: *In Consecratione Episcopali impositionem manuum fieri licet ab omnibus Episcopis praesentibus (76).*

DIOCESAN LITURGICAL LIFE AROUND, should be esteemed by all: *omnes vitam liturgicam dioeceseos circa Episcopum, praesertim in ecclesia cathedrali, maximi faciant oportet (41).*

PASTOR SUBSTITUTES FOR, because it is impossible for him to preside always and everywhere over the whole flock in his Church: *Cum Episcopus in Ecclesia sua ipsemet nec semper nec ubique universo gregi praeesse possit, necessario constituere debet fidelium coetus, inter quos* paroeciae, localiter sub pastore vices gerente Episcopi ordinatae, eminent *(42)*.

BISHOP'S CONFERENCES, CONCELEBRATION AT, is permitted: facultatem concelebrandi . . . concilio extendere placuit: Conventibus Episcopalibus *(57:1.1.b)*.

BISHOPS, DEVOTIONS OF PARTICULAR CHURCHES PRESCRIBED BY, enjoy a special dignity: Speciali quoque dignitate gaudent sacra Ecclesiarum particularium exercititia, quas de mandato Episcoporum celebrantur *(13)*.

BISHOPS, DUTIES AND RIGHTS OF, TO APPOINT DIRECTOR OF TELEVISION AND RADIO: Transmissiones actionum sacrarum ope radiophonica et televisifica, praesertim si agatur de Sacro faciendo, discrete ac decore fiant, ductu et sponsione personae idoneae, ad hoc munus ab Episcopis destinatae *(20)*.

TO AUTHORIZE PERSONS TO PRESIDE OVER BIBLE SERVICES, in places without a priest: Foveatur sacra Verbi Dei celebratio . . . maxime in locis quae sacerdote carent: quo in casu celebrationem diaconus vel alius ab Episcopo delegatus dirigat *(35.4)*.

TO BE CONSULTED BY NATIONAL CONFERENCE OF BISHOPS, with regard to the use of the vernacular if it seems called for: si casus ferat, consilio habito cum Episcopis finitimarum regionum eiusdem linguae, de uso et modo linguae vernaculae statuere *(36:3)*.

TO BE CONSULTED IN THE REVISION OF THE LITURGICAL BOOKS: Libri liturgici quam primum recognoscantur, peritis adhibitis et Episcopis consultis ex diversis orbis regionibus *(25)*.

TO ENCOURAGE PARTICIPATION IN SUNG MASS, which is the right of the faithful as laid down in Art. 28 and 30: Episcopi . . . curent ut in qualibet actione sacra in cantu peragenda universus fidelium coetus actuosam participationem sibi propriam praestare valeat, ad normam art. 28 et 30 *(114)*.

TO ESTABLISH A DIOCESAN COMMISSION FOR THE LITURGY, for promoting the liturgical apostolate: *in singulis dioecesibus Commissio de sacra Liturgia habeatur, ad actionem liturgicam, moderante Episcopo, promovendam (45).*

TO ESTABLISH A DIOCESAN COMMISSION FOR MUSIC, as far as possible: *in quavis dioecesis constituatur, quantum fieri potest, Commissionem de Musica sacra (46).*

TO HAVE SPECIAL CONCERN FOR ARTISTS, so as to imbue them with the spirit of sacred art and of the sacred liturgy: *Episcopi vel per se ipsos vel sacerdotes idoneos qui peritia et artis amore praediti sunt, artificum curam habeant, ut eos spiritu Artis sacrae et sacrae Liturgiae imbuant (127).*

TO JUDGE WHEN COMMUNION UNDER BOTH SPECIES MAY BE GRANTED, not only to clerics and religious, but also to the laity: *Communio sub utraque specie . . . tum clericis et religiosis, tum laicis concedi potest, de iudicio Episcoporum (55).*

TO REGULATE WORSHIP, as the laws may determine: *Sacrae Liturgiae moderatio ab Ecclesiae auctoritate unice pendet: quae quidem est apud Apostolicam Sedem et, ad normam iuris, apud Episcopum (22:1).*

TO WATCH OVER SACRED ART, being careful to remove from the house of God and other sacred places those works which are repugnant to faith, morals, and Christian piety: *Curent Episcopi ut artificum opera, quae fidei et moribus, ac christianae pietati repugnent, offendantque sensum vere religiosum vel ob formarum depravationem . . . ab aedibus Dei aliisque locis sacris sedulo arceantur (124).*

BISHOPS, NATIONAL CONFERENCE OF, TO ADAPT MATERIALS AND FORMS OF SACRED FURNISHINGS AND VESTMENTS, according to the needs and customs of their different regions: *praesertim quoad materiam et formam sacrae supellectilis et indumentorum, territorialibus Episco-*

porum Coetibus facultas tribuitur res aptandi necessitatibus et moribus locorum, ad normam art. 22 huius Constitutionis (128).

TO APPROVE VERNACULAR TRANSLATIONS, for use in the liturgy: *Conversio textus latini in linguam vernaculam in Liturgia adhibenda, a competenti auctoritate ecclesiastica territoriali . . . approbari debet (36:4).*

TO DRAW UP ITS OWN MARRIAGE RITE, suited to the usages of place and people, according to the provision of Art. 63: *competenti auctoritati ecclesiasticae territoriali, de qua in art. 22:2 huius Constitutionis, relinquitur facultas, ad normam art. 63, exarandi ritum proprium usibus locorum et populorum congruentem (77).*

TO ESTABLISH A LITURGICAL COMMISSION, to regulate pastoral-liturgical action throughout the territory, and to promote studies and experiments: *A competenti auctoritate ecclesiastica territoriali, de qua in art. 22:2, expedit ut instituatur Commissio liturgica . . . actionem pastoralem liturgicam in sua dicione moderari, et studia atque necessaria experimenta promovere (44).*

TO JUDGE THE APPROPRIATENESS OF ELEMENTS AND TRADITIONS OF INDIVIDUAL PEOPLES TO BE ADMITTED into divine worship: *A competenti auctoritate ecclesiastica territoriali, de qua in art. 22:2, sedulo et prudenter consideretur quid, hoc in negotio, ex traditionibus ingenioque singulorum populorum opportune in cultum divinum admitti possit (40.1).*

TO PERMIT AND DIRECT PRELIMINARY EXPERIMENTS OF ADAPTATIONS, of the customs and traditions of individual peoples that may be admitted into worship: *Ut autem aptatio cum necessaria circumspectione fiat, eidem auctoritati ecclesiasticae territoriali ab Apostolica Sede facultas tribuetur, si casus ferat, ut in quibusdam coetibus ad id aptis et per determinatum tempus necessaria praevia experimenta permittat et dirigat (40.2).*

TO PREPARE PARTICULAR RITUALS, in harmony with the

new edition of the Roman Ritual: *Iuxta novam Ritualis romani editionem, Ritualia particularia, singularum regionum necessitatibus, etiam quoad linguam, accommodata, a competenti ecclesiastica auctoritate territoriali de qua in art. 22:2 huius Constitutionis quam primum parentur (63.b).*

TO REGULATE USE OF MUSICAL INSTRUMENTS which may be admitted for use in divine worship: *Alia vero instrumenta, de iudicio et consensu auctoritatis territorialis competentis, ad normam art. 22:2, 37 et 40, in cultum divinum admittere licet (120).*

TO REGULATE USE OF THE VERNACULAR, in the liturgy: *est competentis auctoritatis ecclesiasticae territorialis, de qua in art. 22:2 . . . de usu et modo linguae vernaculae statuere (36.3).*

TO REGULATE WORSHIP, in virtue of the power conceded by law within certain defined limits: *Ex potestate a iure concessa rei liturgicae moderatio inter limites statutos pertinet quoque ad competentes varii generis territoriales Episcoporum legitime constitutos (22:2).*

TO SPECIFY THE ADAPTATIONS IN THE LITURGICAL BOOKS, especially in the case of the sacraments, sacramentals, processions, liturgical language, music, and the arts: *Intra limites in editionibus typicis librorum liturgicorum statutos, erit competentis auctoritatis ecclesiasticae territorialis, de qua in art. 22:2, aptationes definire, praesertim quoad administrationem Sacramentorum, quoad Sacramentalia, processiones, linguam liturgicam, musicam sacram et artes, iuxta tamen normas fundamentales quae hac in Constitutione habentur (30).*

TO SUBMIT ADAPTATIONS JUDGED USEFUL TO THE APOSTOLIC SEE, by whose consent they may be introduced: *Aptationes, quae utiles vel necessariae existimantur, Apostolicae Sedi proponantur, de ipsius consensu introducendae (40.1).*

BISHOPS, RESERVED BLESSINGS SHALL BE RESTRICTED ONLY
TO, or ordinaries: *Benedictiones reservatae . . . in favorem tantum Episcoporum vel Ordinariorum (79)*.

BLESSING, NUPTIAL, OUTSIDE OF MASS, always to be given:
*si vero Sacramentum Matrimonii sine Missa celebratur
. . . benedictio sponsis semper impertiatur (78)*.

BLESSED SACRAMENT. See EUCHARIST.

BREVIARY. See DIVINE OFFICE.

BURIAL, RITE OF, should express more clearly the paschal
character of Christian death, and should correspond more
closely to the circumstances and traditions found in various regions. This holds good also for the liturgical color
to be used: *ritus exsequiarum paschalem mortis christianae indolem manifestius exprimat, atque condicionibus
et traditionibus singularum regionum, etiam quoad colorem liturgicum, melius respondeat (81)*.

OF INFANTS, to be revised and a special Mass for the occasion should be provided: *recognoscatur ritus sepeliendi
parvulos, ac propria Missa donetur.*

CALENDAR, DATE OF EASTER IN, could be assigned to a
particular Sunday, provided that those whom it may concern give their consent: *Sacrosanctum Concilium non
obnititur quin festum Paschalis certae dominicae in Calendario Gregoriano assignetur, assentientibus iis quorum
intersit, praesertim fratribus ab Apostolicae Sedis communione seiunctis (Appendix 1)*.

STABILIZATION OF, into civil society not opposed by the
Council: *Sacrosanctum Concilium declarat se non obsistere inceptis quae conferant ad calendarium perpetuum in societatem civilem inducendum (Appendix
2)*.

CATECHUMENATE FOR ADULTS, to be restored:
Instauretur catechumenatus adultorum (64).

CEREMONIES, LITURGICAL, SPECIAL HONORS PROHIBITED
IN, to any persons or classes of persons except those indicated by law: *in Liturgia . . . praeter honores ad normam legum liturgicarum . . . nulla privatarum personarum aut condicionum, sive in caerimoniis, sive in exterioribus pompis, habeatur acceptio (32).*

CHANT. See MUSIC.

CHOIRS, must be diligently promoted in cathedral
churches: *Scholae cantorum assidue provehantur, praesertim apud ecclesias cathedrales (114).* See also MUSIC.

CHRIST, PRIESTHOOD OF, exercised in the liturgy: *Liturgia
habetur veluti Iesu Christi sacerdotalis muneris exercitatio, in qua per signa sensibilia significatur et modo singulis
proprio efficitur sanctificatio hominis (7).*

CHRISTIAN SPIRIT, PRIMARY AND INDISPENSABLE
SOURCE OF, is the liturgy: *est enim primus, isque necessarius fons, et quo spiritum vere christianum fideles hauriant (14).*

CHRISTIANS, ACTIVE PARTICIPATION OF, can be facilitated by their understanding of the texts and rites: *Qua
quidem instauratione, textus et ritus ita ordinari oportet,
ut sancta, quae significant, clarius exprimant, eaque populus christianus, in quantum fieri potest, facile percipere
atque plena, actuosa et communitatis propria celebratione
participare possit (21).*

PERSONAL DEVOTION OF, is not underestimated: *Christianus . . . nihilominus debet etiam intrare in cubiculum suum ut Patrem in abscondito oret, immo, docente
Apostolo, sine intermissione orare (12).*

POPULAR DEVOTIONS OF, are highly recommended, provided they are in accord with the laws and norms of the
Church: *Pia populi christiani exercitia, dummodo legibus et normis Ecclesiae conformia sint (13).*

PURPOSE OF REFORM AND, that they may derive an abundance of graces from the liturgy: *Pia Mater Ecclesia,
ut populus christianus in sacra Liturgia abundantiam*

gratiarum securius assequatur, ipsius Liturgiae generalem instaurationem sedulo curare cupit (21).

SPIRITUAL LIFE OF, not limited solely to participation in
the liturgy: *Vita tamen spiritualis non unius sacrae
Liturgiae participatione continetur* (12).

CHURCH, ADORNMENT, she has been particularly careful
to see that sacred furnishings should worthily and beauti-
fully serve the dignity of worship: *Peculiari sedulitate
Ecclesia curavit ut sacra supellex digne et pulchre cultus
decori inserviret* (122).

ART AND, always fostered and admitted into worship:
*Mater Ecclesia proinde semper fuit ingenuarum artium
amica, earumque nobile ministerium* (122).

BLESSED MOTHER AND, her devotion occupies a distinctive
place in the liturgical year: *In hoc annuo mysteriorum
Christi circulo celebrando, Sancta Mater Ecclesia
Beatam Mariam Dei Genetricem cum peculiari amore
veneratur* (103).

BRIDE OF CHRIST, who calls to her Lord, and through Him
offers worship to the Eternal Father: *Christus Ecclesiam, sponsam suam dilectissimam, sibi semper consociat, quae Dominum suum invocat et per ipsum
Aeterno Patri cultum tribuit* (7).

CHRIST IS PRESENT IN, especially in her liturgical celebrations. He is present in the Mass, especially under the
eucharistic species. By His power He is present in the
sacraments . . . He is present in His word . . . He is
present, lastly, when the Church prays and sings:
*Christus Ecclesiae suae semper adest, praesertim in
actionibus liturgicis. Praesens in Missae . . . tum
maxime sub speciebus eucharisticis. Praesens adest virtute sua in Sacramentis . . . Praesens adest in verbo
suo . . . Praesens adest denique dum supplicat et psallit Ecclesia* (7).

CONTEMPORARY ART AND, is given free scope, provided
that it adorns the sacred buildings and holy rites with
due reverence and honor: *Nostrorum etiam temporum*

atque omnium gentium et regionum ars liberum in Ecclesia exercitium habeat, dummodo sacris aedibus sacrisque ritibus debita reverentia debitoque honore inserviat (123).

DESIRE OF, that all the faithful be led to an intelligent
and active participation in liturgical celebrations: *Valde
cupit Mater Ecclesia ut fideles universi ad plenam illam,
consciam atque actuosam liturgicarum celebrationum
participationem ducantur (14).*

that the faithful, when present at the Eucharistic Sacrifice, should not be there as strangers or silent spectators; on the contrary, they should intelligently participate: *Itaque Ecclesia sollicitas curas eo intendit
ne christifideles huic fidei mysterio tamquam extranei
vel muti spectatores intersint, sed per ritus et preces
id bene intellegentes, sacram actionem conscie, pie
et actuose participent (48).*

that the rites, where necessary, be revised carefully in
the light of sound tradition, and that they be given
new vigor to meet the circumstances and needs of
modern times: *optat ut, ubi opus sit, caute ex integro
ad mentem sanae traditionis recognoscantur, et novo
vigore, pro hodiernis adiunctus et necessitatibus,
donentur (4).*

to preserve all lawfully acknowledged rites in the future
and to foster them in every way: *Sanctam Matrem
Ecclesiam omnes ritus legitime agnitos . . . eosque
in posterum servari et omnimodo foveri velle (4).*

FULFILLS HER MISSION, not only by celebrating the Eucharist, but also in other ways, especially by praying the
Divine Office: *Illud enim sacerdotale munus per ipsam
suam Ecclesiam pergit, quae non tantum Eucharistia
celebranda, sed etiam aliis modis, praesertim Officio
divino persolvendo (83).*

INTERCESSION ON BEHALF OF, is to be made in the restored
"common prayer" of the Mass: *"Orationes communis"
. . . pro sancta Ecclesia (53).*

LAWFULLY ACKNOWLEDGED RITES AND, considered as being of equal right and dignity: *Sanctam Matrem Ecclesiam omnes ritus legitime agnitos aequo iure atque honore habere (4).*

LIFE OF, is manifested in zeal for the promotion and restoration of the liturgy: *Sacrae Liturgiae fovendae atque instaurandae studium merito habetur veluti signum providentialium dispositionum Dei . . . et vitam ipsius . . . nota propria distinguit (43).*

LITURGICAL AUTHORITY OF, depends solely on the Apostolic See and, as laws may determine, on the bishop: *Sacrae Liturgiae moderatio ab Ecclesiae auctoritate unice pendet: quae quidem est apud Apostolicam Sedem et, ad normam iuris, apud Episcopum (22:1).*

LITURGICAL CELEBRATIONS OF, pertain to the whole body of the Church: *Quare ad universum Corpus Ecclesiae pertinent (26).*

MESSENGER OF SALVATION, she announces the good tidings to those who do not believe . . . To believers she must ever preach faith and penance, prepare them for the sacraments, teach them to observe what Christ has commanded, invite them to works of charity: *Quare Ecclesia non credentibus praeconium salutis annuntiat . . . Credentibus vero semper fidem et paenitentiam praedicare debet, eos praeterea debet ad Sacramenta disponere, docere servare omnia quaecumque mandavit Christus, et allicere ad omnia opera caritatis (9).*

MUSICAL TRADITION OF, is of inestimable value: *Musica traditio Ecclesiae universae thesaurum constituit pretii inaestimabilis (112).*

NATURE OF, it is of her very essence to be both human and divine, visible and yet invisibly equipped: *Ecclesiae naturam . . . cuius proprium est esse humanam simul ac divinam, visibilem invisibilibus praeditam (2).*

PREEMINENT MANIFESTATION OF, consists in the full active participation of the faithful in liturgical celebrations: *praecipuam manifestationem Ecclesiae haberi in*

plenaria et actuosa participatione totius plebis sanctae
Dei in iisdem celebrationibus liturgicis (41).

PROLONGS PRIESTLY WORK OF CHRIST, which is ceaselessly
engaged in praising the Lord and interceding for the
salvation of the whole world: *Illud enim sacerdotale
munus per ipsam suam Ecclesiam pergit . . . Dominum sine intermissione laudat et pro totius mundi
salute interpellat (83).*

SAINTS AND MARTYRS AND, their veneration occupies a
place in the liturgical year: *Memorias insuper Martyrum aliorumque Sanctorum . . . circulo anni inseruit Ecclesia (104).*

STYLES OF ART AND, have been given freedom of expression. She accepts them from every period according to
the natural talents and circumstances of peoples, and
the needs of the various rites: *Ecclesia nullum artis
stilum veluti proprium habuit, sed secundum gentium
indoles ac condiciones atque variorum Rituum necessitates modos cuiusvis aetatis admisit (123).*

TWOFOLD MISSION OF, the glory of God and the sanctification of men: *Christus Ecclesiam, sponsam suam dilectissimam, sibi semper consociat . . . Reapse tanto
in opere, quo Deus perfecte glorificatur, et homines
sanctificantur (7).*

WHOLE MYSTERY OF CHRIST UNFOLDED BY, in the cycle
of a year: *totum vero Christi mysterium per anni circulum explicat (102).*

CHURCH BUILDINGS, LAWS FOR CONSTRUCTING, to be
revised: *canones et statuta ecclesiastica quae spectant
praesertim quoad aedium sacrarum dignam et aptam
constructionem . . . quam primum recognoscantur
(128).*

SUITABILITY OF, for the celebration of the liturgy and
active participation of the faithful is to be achieved
when they are to be built: *In aedificandis vero sacris
aedibus, diligenter curetur ut ad liturgicas actiones ex-*

sequendas *et ad fidelium actuosam participationem obtinendam idoneae sint (124).*

CHURCH FURNISHINGS, ALL STYLES OF, materials, and ornamentation are admitted according to the times and progress of the technical arts: *sacra supellex . . . eas mutationes sive in materia, sive in forma, sive in ornatu admittens, quas artis technicae progressus per temporis decursum invexit (122).*

> LAWS ON, to be revised: *Canones et statuta ecclesiastica, quae rerum externarum ad sacrum cultum pertinentium apparatum spectant . . . quam primum recognoscantur (128).*

> OUTMODED LAWS ON, to be brought into harmony with the reformed liturgy, or else abolished: *quae liturgiae instauratae minus congruere videntur, emendentur aut aboleantur (128).*

CHURCH MUSIC. See MUSIC.

CHURCH YEAR. See YEAR, LITURGICAL.

CHURCHES, ARRANGEMENT OF STATUES IN, must reflect a right order: *in ecclesiis sacras imagines . . . congruo ordine exponantur (125).*

> IMAGES AND STATUES IN, their use is to be maintained: *Firma maneat praxis, in ecclesiis sacras imagines fidelium venerationi proponendi (125).*

> LAWS FOR ARRANGING STATUES IN, to be revised: *Canones et statuta ecclesiastica . . . congruentem sacrarum imaginum . . . quam primum recognoscantur (128).*

> LIMITATION OF STATUES IN, their number is to be moderate: *in ecclesiis sacras imagines . . . moderato numero (125).*

CIVIL AUTHORITIES, HONORS FOR, are provided in liturgical laws: *In Liturgia . . . praeter honores ad normam legum liturgicarum auctoritatibus civilibus debitos (32).*

> INTERCESSION ON BEHALF OF, is to be made in the restored "common prayer" of the Mass: *"Oratio communis"*

. . . *obsecrationes fiant . . . pro iis qui nos in po-*
testate regunt (53).

CIVIL SOCIETY, PERPETUAL CALENDAR IN, would not be
opposed by the Council, on the condition that it retain
and safeguard a seven-day week with Sunday, without the
introduction of any days outside the week, so that the suc-
cession of weeks may be left intact: *Sacrosanctum Con-*
cilium declarat se non obsistere inceptis quae conferant
ad calendarium perpetuum in societatem civilem inducen-
dum (Appendix 1). Variorum autem systematum . . .
iis tantum Ecclesia non obsistit, quae hebdomadam sep-
tum dierum cum dominica servant et tutantur, nullis
diebus extra hebdomadam septem dierum interiectis, ita
ut hebdomadarum successio intacta (Appendix 2).

CLERGY, CONFERENCES, CONCELEBRATION AT, is allowed:
facultatem concelebrandi . . . extendere placuit ad
Missas in conventibus cuiusvis generis sacerdotum tum
saecularium tum religiosorum (51:1.2.b).

> NEED FOR UNDERSTANDING OF LITURGY, they are to be
> helped by every suitable means to know what it is they
> are doing when they perform the sacred rites: *Sacer-*
> *dotes, sive saeculares sive religiosi in vinea Domini iam*
> *operantes, omnibus mediis opportunis iuventur ut*
> *semper quae in functionibus sacris agunt intellegant*
> *(18).*

CLERICS, NEED FOR LITURGICAL FORMATION OF, in seminaries and houses of religious: *Clerici, in seminariis*
domibusque religiosis, formationem vitae spiritualis li-
turgicam acquirant (17).

> NEED FOR LITURGICAL TRAINING OF, so that they may be
> able to understand the sacred rites and take part in
> them wholeheartedly: *cum apta manductione qua*
> *sacros ritus intellegere et toto animo participare queant*
> *(17).*

> TO OBSERVE LITURGICAL LAWS, so that life in seminaries
> and houses of religious may be thoroughly influenced

by the spirit of the liturgy: *observantiam legum liturgicarum addiscant, ita ut vita seminariis et religiosorum institutis liturgico spiritu penitus informetur* (17).

COLOR, LITURGICAL, to be adapted in the rite of burial of dead according to the circumstances and traditions found in various regions: *Ritus exsequiarum . . . condicionibus et traditionibus singularum regionum, etiam quoad colorem liturgicum* (81).

COMMENTARIES, LITURGICAL, can be given in a variety of ways; if necessary, short directives to be spoken by the priest or proper minister within the rites themselves: *catechesis directius liturgica omnibus modis inculcetur; et in ipsis ritibus, si necessariae sint, breves admonitiones, a sacerdote vel competenti ministro* (35.3).

PROPER TIME FOR, they should occur within the rites, only during the more suitable moments: *opportunioribus tantum momentis* (35.3).

TEXTS OF, should be in the prescribed words of the rites themselves or similar words: *praescriptis vel similibus verbis, dicendae* (35.3).

COMMENTATORS, exercise a genuine liturgical function: *commentatores . . . vero ministerio liturgico funguntur* (29).

TO BE TRAINED, to perform their function in a correct and orderly manner, and be imbued with the spirit of the liturgy: *oportet eos spiritu Liturgiae, suo cuiusque modo, sedulo imbui, et ad partes suas rite et ordinate obeundas institui* (29).

COMMISSION, DIOCESAN, FOR LITURGY, to be established: *in singulis diocesibus Commissio de sacra Liturgia habeatur, ad actionem liturgicam moderante Episcopo, promovendam* (45).

FOR SACRED ART, to be established: *in quavis dioecesi constituatur quantum fieri potest, etiam Commissionem . . . de Arte sacra* (46).

FOR SACRED MUSIC, to be established: *in quavis dioecesi constituatur, quantum fieri potest, etiam Commissionem de Musica sacra (46)*.

UNITED, FOR THE LITURGY, may be established between several dioceses if they find it expedient: *opportunum aliquando evadere potest ut plures dioeceses unam Commissionem constituant, quae, collatis consiliis, rem liturgicam provehat (45)*.

COMMISSION, TERRITORIAL, FOR LITURGY, to be established by the competent territorial ecclesiastical authority mentioned in Art. 22:2: *A competenti auctoritate ecclesiastica territoriali, de qua in art. 22:2, expedit ut instituatur Commissio liturgica, a viris in scientia liturgica, Musica, Arte sacra ac re pastorali peritis iuvanda (44)*.

DUTY OF, to regulate, under the direction of the territorial ecclesiastical authority the pastoral-liturgical action throughout the territory, and to promote studies and necessary experiments whenever there is question of adaptations to be proposed to the Apostolic See: *Ipsius Commissionis erit, ductu auctoritatis ecclesiasticae territorialis . . . et actionem pastoralem liturgicam in sua dicione moderari, et studia atque necessaria a experimenta promovere, quoties agatur de aptationibus Apostolicae Sedi proponendis (44)*.

COMMISSIONS, DIOCESAN, FOR LITURGY, ART, MUSIC, must collaborate and sometimes it might be best to fuse the three of them into one single commission: *Necessarium est ut hae tres Commissiones consociatis viribus adlaborent; immo non raro congruum erit ut in unam Commissionem coalescant (46)*.

COMMON PRAYER, AT MASS, AIM OF, to intercede for holy Church, for the civil authorities, for those oppressed by various needs, for all mankind, and for the salvation of the entire world: *obsecrationes fiant pro sancta Ecclesia, pro iis qui nos in potestate regunt, pro iis qui variis*

premuntur necessitatibus, ac pro omnibus hominibus totiusque mundi salute *(53)*.

PARTICIPATION IN, by all the people: *populo eam participante (53)*.

TO BE RESTORED, especially on Sundays and feasts of obligation: "*Oratio communis*" *seu* "*fidelium*" . . . *praesertim dominicis et festis de praecepto, restituatur (53)*.

VERNACULAR IN, is allowed: *Linguae vernaculae in Missis
cum populo celebratis congruus locus tribui possit,
praesertim* . . . "*oratione communi*" *(54)*.

COMMUNAL CELEBRATION OF LITURGY, RITES
THAT PROVIDE FOR, are preferred: *Quoties ritus, iuxta
propriam cuiusque naturam, secum ferunt celebrationem
communem, cum frequentia et actuosa participatione
fidelium* . . . *in quantum fieri potest, esse praeferendam
celebrationi eorundem singulari et quasi privatae (27)*.

OF MASS AND SACRAMENTS, RITES THAT PROVIDE FOR, are
especially preferred: *Quoties ritus, iuxta propriam
cuiusque naturam, secum ferunt celebrationem communem* . . . *esse praeferendam* . . . *Quod valet
praesertim pro Missae celebratione, salve semper natura
publica et sociali cuiusvis Missae, et pro Sacramentorum administratione (27)*.

COMMUNION. See EUCHARIST, COMMUNION.

COMMUNITY, SENSE OF, to be encouraged within the
parish, especially in the common celebration of the Sunday Mass: *adlaborandum ut sensus communitatis paroecialis, imprimis vero in communi celebratione Missae
dominicalis (42)*.

COMPLINE, to be revised: *Completorium ita instruatur,
ut fini diei apte conveniat (89.b)*.

COMPOSERS OF SACRED MUSIC, to be guided by religion: *Sentiant musicae artifices, spiritu christiano imbuti, se ad Musicam sacram colendam et ad thesaurum
eius augendum esse vocatos (121)*.

COMPOSITIONS OF, to be suitable not only for larger choirs, but also small choirs and for the active participation of the entire assembly of the faithful: *Modos autem componant . . . non solum a maioribus scholis cantorum cani possint, sed minoribus quoque scholis conveniant et actuosam participationem totius coetus fidelium foveant (121).*

TEXTS USED BY, are to be in conformity with Catholic doctrine; indeed they should be drawn chiefly from holy Scripture and from liturgical sources: *Textus cantui sacro destinati catholicae sint conformes, immo ex Sacris Scripturis et fontibus liturgicis potissimum hauriantur (121).*

CONCELEBRATION, BY MEANS OF, unity of the priesthood is appropriately manifested: *Concelebratio, qua unitas sacerdotii opportune manifestatur (57:1).*

NEW RITE FOR, to be drawn up and inserted into the Pontifical and into the Roman Missal: *Novus ritus concelebrationis conficiatur, Pontificali et Missali Romano inserendus (58).*

PERMISSION FOR, is granted in the following cases:
1. a) on the Thursday of the Lord's Supper, not only at the Mass of the Chrism, but also at the evening Mass;
   b) at Masses during councils, bishops' conferences, and synods;
   c) at the Mass for the blessing of an abbot.
2. Also, with permission of the ordinary, to whom it belongs to decide whether concelebration is opportune:
   a) at conventual Mass, and at the principal Mass in churches when the needs of the faithful do not require that all the priests available should celebrate individually;
   b) at Masses celebrated at any kind of priests' meetings, whether the priests be secular clergy or religious.

Facultatem concelebrandi ad sequentes casus Concilio extendere placuit:

1. a) *feria V in Cena Domini, tum ad Missam chrismatis, tum ad Missam vespertinam;*
   b) *ad Missas in Conciliis, Conventibus Episcopalibus et Synodis;*
   c) *ad Missam in Benedictione Abbatis.*
2. *Praeterea, accedente licentia Ordinarii, cuius est de opportunitate concelebrationis iudicare:*
   a) *ad Missam conventualem et ad Missam principalem in ecclesiis, cum utilitas christifidelium singularem celebrationem omnium sacerdotum praesentium non postulat;*
   b) *ad Missas in conventibus cuiusvis generis sacerdotum tum saecularium tum religiosorum* (57:1).

CONFERENCE, BISHOPS', CONCELEBRATION is allowed: *ad Missas in conventibus Episcopalibus et Synodis* (57:1. 1.b).

PRIESTS', CONCELEBRATION is allowed: *ad Missas in conventibus cuiusvis generis sacerdotum tum saecularium tum religiosorum* (57:1.2.b).

CONFESSION. See PENANCE, SACRAMENT OF.

CONFIRMATION, OUTSIDE OF MASS, the rite to be used should be introduced by a formula drawn up for this purpose: *Confirmatio . . . ad ritum autem extra Missam quod attinet, paretur formula ad modum introductionis adhibenda* (71).

RENEWAL OF BAPTISMAL VOWS BEFORE, is recommended: *Ritus Confirmationis . . . quapropter renovatio promissionum Baptismi convenienter ipsam Sacramenti susceptionem praecedet* (71).

RITE OF, to be revised: *Ritus Confirmationis recognoscatur* (71).

WITHIN MASS, is allowed when convenient: *Confirmatio pro opportunitate, intra Missam conferri potest* (71).

CONGREGATIONAL SINGING, to be skilfully fostered
in liturgical functions: *Cantus popularis religiosus sollerter foveatur, ita ut in piis sacrisque exercitiis et in ipsis
liturgicis actionibus . . . (118).*

    IN MASS, to be made possible so that the faithful may be
able to contribute that active participation which is
rightly theirs: *Episcopi vero ceterique animarum pastores sedulo curent ut in qualibet actione sacra in cantu
peragenda universus fidelium coetus actuosam participationem sibi propriam praestare valeat, ad normam
art. 28 et 30 (114).*

CONSECRATION OF BISHOP, ALLOCUTION IN RITE OF,
may be in the vernacular: *Allocutiones Episcopi, initio
cuiusque Ordinationis aut Consecrationis, fieri possunt
lingua vernacula (76).*

    IMPOSITION OF HANDS IN, may be done by all bishops pres-
ent: *In Consecratione Episcopali impositionem manuum fieri licet ab omnibus Episcopis praesentibus
(76).*

CONSECRATION OF VIRGINS, RITE OF, to be revised:
*Ritus Consecrationis Virginum, qui in Pontificali romano
habetur, recognitioni subiciatur (80).*

CONVENTUAL MASS, CONCELEBRATION, is allowed with
permission of the ordinary: *concelebratio . . . accedente
licentia Ordinarii . . . ad Missam conventualem (57:1.
2.a).*

    OBLIGATION TO CELEBRATE, by communities bound to
celebrate office in choir every day: *Communitates choro
obligatae . . . Missam conventualem, tenentur . . .
cotidie celebrare (95).*

CONVERTS. See BAPTISM, CONVERTS.

COUNCIL, VATICAN II, AIM OF, to impart an ever increasing vigor to the Christian life of the faithful; to adapt
more suitably to the needs of our own times those institutions which are subject to change; to foster whatever can
promote union among all who believe in Christ; to

strengthen whatever can help to call the whole of mankind into the household of the Church: *Sacrosanctum Concilium cum sibi proponant vitam christianam inter fideles in dies augere; eas institutiones quae mutationibus obnoxiae sunt, ad nostrae aetatis necessitates melius accommodare; quidquid ad unionem omnium in Christum credentium conferre potest, fovere; et quidquid ad omnes in sinum Ecclesiae vocandos conducit, roborare (1).*

COUNCILS, CONCELEBRATION AT, is allowed: *facultatem concelebrandi . . . ad Missas in Conciliis (57:1.1.b).*

CUSTOMS, ART, all styles are adopted according to periods, natural talents and circumstances of peoples, and the needs of the various rites: *Ecclesia nullum artis stilum veluti proprium habuit sed secundum gentium indoles ac condiciones atque variorum Rituum necessitates modos cuiusvis aetatis admisit (123).*

INITIATION RITES IN MISSIONS, elements which are capable of being adapted to Christian ritual may be admitted along with those already found in Christian tradition: *In terris Missionum, praeter ea quae in traditione christiana habentur, illa etiam elementa initiationis admitti liceat, quae apud unumquemque populum in usu esse reperiuntur, quatenus ritui christiano accommodari possunt (65).*

LENTEN PRACTICES, to be fostered in ways that are possible in our own times and in different regions, and according to the circumstances of the faithful: *Praxis paenitentialis, iuxta nostrae aetatis et diversarum regionum possibilitates necnon fidelium condiciones, foveatur (110).*

LITURGICAL BOOKS, provisions to be made for legitimate variations and adaptations to different groups, regions, and peoples, especially in mission lands: *legitimis varietatibus et aptationibus ad diversos coetus, regiones, populos, praesertim in Missionibus, locus relinquatur, etiam cum libri liturgici (38).*

LITURGICAL YEAR, to be revised so that the traditional customs and discipline of the sacred seasons be preserved or restored to suit the conditions of modern times: *Annus liturgicus ita recognoscatur, ut servatis aut restitutis sacrorum temporum traditis consuetudinibus et disciplinis iuxta nostrae aetatis condiciones, ipsorum indoles nativa retineatur (107).*

LITURGY, the Church respects and fosters the genius and talents of the various races and peoples . . . if possible she admits such things into the liturgy: *Ecclesia . . . variarum gentium populorumque animi ornamenta ac dotes colit et provehit; . . si potest . . in ipsam Liturgiam admittit (37).*

MUSIC IN MISSION LANDS, may play a great part in the religious and social life of the peoples. A suitable place is to be given to their music: *Cum in regionibus quibusdam, praesertim Missionum, gentes inveniantur quibus propria est traditio musica, magnum momentum in earum vita religiosa ac sociali habens, huic . . . locus congruus praebeatur (119).*

REGULATION OF ADAPTATIONS, after prudent and careful consideration by the competent territorial ecclesiastical authority, to be then submitted to the Apostolic See, by whose consent they may be introduced: *A competenti auctoritate ecclesiastica territoriali, de qua in art. 22:2, sedulo et prudenter consideretur quid . . . aptationes . . . Apostolicae Sedi proponantur, de ipsius consensu introducendae (40.1).*

RITE OF BURIAL, should correspond more closely to the circumstances and traditions found in various regions: *Ritus exsequiarum . . . condicionibus et traditionibus singularum regionum . . . melius respondeat (81).*

SACRED FURNISHINGS, the territorial bodies of bishops are empowered to adapt the materials and form according to the needs and customs of different regions: *praesertim quoad materiam et formam sacrae supellectilis et indumentorum, territorialibus Episcoporum Coetibus* facultas tribuitur res aptandi necessitatibus et moribus locorum *(128)*.

CYCLE, ANNUAL, THE FORMATION OF FAITHFUL AND, is completed by means of pious practices for soul and body, by instruction, prayer, and works of penance and of mercy: *Variis denique anni temporibus iuxta traditas disciplinas, Ecclesia fidelium eruditionem perficit, per pias animi et corporis exercitationes, instructionem, precationem paenitentiae et misericordiae opera (105).*

DEACON, BIBLE SERVICES AND, to preside over the celebration in places without a priest: *sacra Verbi Dei celebratio . . . maxime in locis quae sacerdote carent: quo in casu celebrationem diaconus vel alius ab Episcopo delegatus dirigat (35.4).*

DEAD, RITE FOR BURIAL OF, to be adapted according to the circumstances and traditions of the various regions: *Ritus exsequiarum . . . condicionibus et traditionibus singularum regionum, etiam quoad colorem liturgicum, melius respondeat (81).* See also BURIAL; COLOR.

DEVOTIONS, POPULAR, TO BE HIGHLY COMMENDED, provided they accord with the laws and norms of the Church, above all when they are ordered by the Apostolic See: *Pia populi christiana exercitia, dummodo legibus et normis Ecclesiae conformia sint, valde commendantur, praesertim cum de mandato Apostolicae Sedis fiunt (13).*

NOT TO BE NEGLECTED, the Christian is indeed called to pray with his brethren, but he must also enter into his chamber to pray to the Father in secret: *Christianus enim ad communiter orandum vocatus, nihilominus debet etiam intrare in cubiculum suum ut Patrem in abscondito oret (12).*

NOT TO BE UNDERESTIMATED, the spiritual life is not limited solely to participation in the liturgy: *Vita tamen spiritualis non unius sacrae Liturgiae participatione continetur (12).*

PROPER TO INDIVIDUAL CHURCHES, also have a special dignity if they are undertaken by mandate of the bishops according to customs or books lawfully approved: *Speciali quoque dignitate gaudent sacra Ecclesiarum particularium exercitia, quae de mandato Episcoporum celebrantur, secundum consuetudines aut libros legitime approbatos (13).*

DIALOGUE MASS, PARTICIPATION IN, by encouraging the people to take part by means of acclamations, responses, psalmody, antiphons, and songs, as well as by actions, gestures and bodily attitudes: *Ad actuosam participationem promovendam, populi acclamationes, responsiones, psalmodia, antiphonae, cantica, necnon actiones seu gestus et corporis habitus foveantur (30).*

VERNACULAR IN, is allowed, as local conditions may warrant, to those parts which pertain to the people: *Linguae vernaculae in Missis cum populo celebratis . . . pro condicione locorum, etiam in partibus quae ad populum spectant, ad normam art. 36 huius Constitutionis (54).*

DIOCESAN COMMISSION FOR ART, to be established, as far as possible: *in quavis dioecesi constituatur, quantum fieri potest . . . Commissionem de Arte sacra (46).*

FOR LITURGY, to be established under the direction of the bishop: *in singulis dioecesibus Commissio de sacra Liturgia habeatur . . . moderante Episcopo (45).*

FOR MUSIC, to be established, as far as possible: *in quavis dioecesi constituatur, quantum fieri potest . . . Commissionem de Musica sacra (46).*

DIOCESAN COMMISSIONS OF ART, LITURGY, MUSIC, to work in closest collaboration; indeed it will often be best to fuse the three of them into one single commission: *Necessarium est ut hae tres Commissiones consociatis viribus adlaborent; immo non raro congruum erit ut in unam Commissionem coalescant (46).*

DIOCESE, LITURGICAL LIFE OF, to be held by all in great esteem: *omnes vitam liturgicam dioeceseos circa Episcopum, praesertim in ecclesia cathedrali, maximi faciant oportet (41).*

DIVINE AND HUMAN ELEMENTS, CHURCH AND, it is of her very essence that she possess both: *Ecclesiae naturam, cuius proprium est esse humanam simul ac divinam (2).*

DIVINE OFFICE, AIM OF REVISION, so that it may be better and more perfectly prayed in existing circumstances: *Ut autem divinum Officium . . . melius et perfectius in rerum adiunctis peragatur, Sacrosancto Concilio, instaurationem . . . (87).*

ATTENTION AND DEVOTION DEMANDED, since it is the public prayer of the Church, a source of piety and nourishment for personal prayer: *Cum praeterea Officium divinum, utpote oratio publica Ecclesiae, sit fons pietatis et orationis personalis nutrimentum, . . . omnes divinum Officium participantes, ut in eo persolvendo mens concordet voci (90).*

ATTENTION AND DEVOTION FACILITATED, by an understanding of the liturgy and of the Bible, especially of the psalms: *ad quod melius assequendum, liturgicam et biblicam, praecipue psalmorum, institutionem sibi uberiorem comparent (90).*

BENEFITS FOR THE PRIEST AND HIS APOSTOLATE, their work will effect nothing and bring no fruit except by the power of the Lord. They should therefore offer the praises of the hours with greater fervor realizing they must pray without ceasing: *Sacerdotes sacro pastorali ministerio addicti eo maiore fervore Horarum laudes persolvent, quo vividius conscii erunt sibi observandum*

esse monitum Pauli: "Sine intermissione orate" . . .
*operi enim in quo laborant Dominus solus efficacitatem
et incrementum dare potest (86).*

CATHEDRAL OR COLLEGIATE CHAPTERS, have the obligation to celebrate in choir those parts of the Office im-
posed on them by general or particular law: *Capitula
cathedralia vel collegialia, eas partes Officii (in choro),
quae sibi a iure communi vel particulari imponuntur,
celebrare (95.b).*

CHANT IN, when possible it is fitting that it be sung both
in common and in choir: *Praestat insuper ut Officium
in choro et in communi, pro opportunitate, cantetur
(99).*

CHARACTER OF LAUDS, a morning prayer, hence to be considered as one of the chief hours: *Laudes, ut preces
matutinae . . . ex venerabili universae Ecclesiae traditione . . . cardo Officii cotidiani, Horae praecipuae
habendae sunt et ita celebrandae (89.a).*

CHARACTER OF VESPERS, an evening prayer, hence to be
considered as one of the chief hours: *Vesperae, ut
preces vespertinae, ex venerabili universae Ecclesiae traditione . . . cardo Officii cotidiani, Horae praecipuae
habendae sunt et ita celebrandae (89.a).*

CHRIST'S PRIESTLY WORK CONTINUED IN, through the
Church ceaselessly engaged in praising the Lord and
interceding for the salvation of the whole world, especially by praying the Divine Office: *Christus Jesus . . .
illud sacerdotale munus per ipsam suam Ecclesiam
pergit, . . . praesertim Officio divino persolvendo,
Dominum sine intermissione laudat et pro totius
mundi salute interpellat (83).*

COMMON RECITATION ENCOURAGED, for those clerics not
obliged to Office in choir, especially priests who live
together or who assemble for any purpose: *suadetur ut
clerici choro haud obligati ac praesertim sacerdotes con-
viventes vel in unum convenientes, aliquam saltem
divinum Officii partem in communi persolvant (99).*

COMPLINE, to be revised: *Completorium ita instruatur, ut fini diei apte conveniat (89.b).*

DISPENSATION FROM OBLIGATION OF RECITING, can be granted in particular cases and for a just reason by ordinaries, in whole or in part, or this obligation may be commuted: *In casibus singularibus iustaque de causa, Ordinarii possunt subditos suos ab obligatione Officium recitandi ex toto vel ex parte dispensare vel id commutare (97).*

DUTY TO PROPERLY DISCHARGE OBLIGATION OF RECITING, this refers not only to the internal devotion of the mind but also to the external manner of celebration: *Omnes autem sive in choro sive in communi Officium persolventes munus sibi concreditum quam perfectissime, tam interna animi devotione quam externa agendi ratione, peragant (99).*

HOURLY SANCTIFICATION, by tradition the Divine Office is devised so that the whole course of the day and night is made holy by the praises of God: *Divinum Officium ex antiqua traditione christiana ita est constitutum ut totus cursus diei ac noctis per laudem Dei consecretur (84).*

HOURS AT PROPER TIMES, so that the day may be truly sanctified, and the hours themselves be recited with spiritual advantage: *Praestat, sive ad diem revera sanctificandum, sive ad ipsas Horas cum fructu spirituali recitandas, ut in Horarum absolutione tempus servetur, quod proxime accedat ad tempus verum uniuscuiusque Horae canonicae (94).*

HYMNS, to be restored to their original form, and whatever smacks of mythology or ill accords with Christian piety is to be removed or changed: *Hymni, quantum expedire videtur, ad pristinam formam restituantur, iis demptis vel mutatis quae mythologiam sapiunt aut christianae pietati minus congruunt (93).*

LAITY, are encouraged to recite either with the priests, or among themselves, or even individually: *Commendatur*

ut et ipsi laici recitent Officium divinum, vel cum
sacerdotibus vel inter se congregati, quin immo unusquisque solus (100).

LATIN IN, to be retained by clerics: *Iuxta saecularem traditionem ritus latini, in Officio divino lingua latina clericis servanda est (101:1).*

MATINS, to be adapted so that it can be recited at any
hour of the day; it shall be made up of fewer psalms and
longer readings: *Hora quae Matutinum vocatur, . . .
ita accommodetur ut qualibet diei hora recitari possit,
et e psalmis paucioribus lectionibusque longioribus constet (89.c).*

MEMBERS OF COMMUNITIES OBLIGED TO CHORAL RECITA-
TION, who are in major orders or who are solemnly
professed, except for lay brothers, are bound to recite
individually those canonical hours which they do not
pray in choir: *Omnes autem illarum Communitatum
sodales (tenentur Officium cotidie in choro celebrare),
qui sunt aut in Ordinibus maioribus constitui aut solemniter professi, conversis exceptis, debent eas Horas
canonicas soli recitare, quas in choro non persolvunt
(95.c).*

MINOR HOURS IN CHOIR, are to be observed: *In choro,
Horae minores Tertia, Sexta, Nona serventur (89.e).*

MINOR HOURS OUTSIDE CHOIR, it will be lawful to select
any one of the three, according to the respective time
of the day: *Extra chorum e tribus (Tertia, Sexta, Nona)
unam seligere licet, diei tempori magis congruentem
(89.e).*

NEW HYMNS, may be selected and incorporated as the
occasion may arise: *Recipiantur quoque, pro opportunitate, alii qui in hymnorum thesauro inveniuntur (93).*

NON-CLERICAL INSTITUTES, who according to their constitutions, are to recite any part, are thereby performing
the public prayer of the Church: *Sodales cuiusvis Instituti status perfectionis, qui, vi Constitutionum,*

partes aliquas divini Officii absolvunt, orationem publicam Ecclesiae agunt (98).

OBLIGATION OF CLERICS NOT BOUND TO CHORAL RECITA-
TION, if in major orders they must pray the entire office
every day, either in common or individually, as laid
down in Art. 89: *clerici choro non obligati, si sunt in
Ordinibus maioribus constituti, cotidie, sive in communi, sive soli, obligatione tenentur totum Officium
persolvendi, ad normam art. 89 (96).*

OBLIGATION SATISFIED IN THE VERNACULAR, if a cleric who
is bound to the Office, prays it together with a group of
faithful or with those mentioned in 101.2, provided
that the text of the translation is approved: *Quivis
clericus Officio divino adstrictus, si Officium divinum
una cum coetu fidelium, vel cum iis qui sub 101:2 re-
censentur, lingua vernacula celebrat, suae obligationi
satisfacit, dummodo textus versionis sit approbatus
(101:3).*

ORDERS OF CANONS, have the obligation to recite the entire
office in choir: *totum officium, Ordo Canonicorum
. . . choro adstrictorum (95.a).*

ORDERS OF MONKS, have the obligation to recite the entire
office in choir: *totum officium, Ordo Monachorum
. . . choro adstrictorum (95.a).*

ORDERS OF NUNS, have the obligation to recite the entire
office in choir: *totum officium, Ordo Monialium . . .
choro adstrictorum (95.a).*

PRAYER OF THE MYSTICAL BODY, the voice of the entire
Church publicly praising God: *Officium divinum sit
vox Ecclesiae seu totius Corporis mystici Deum publice
laudantis (99).*

PRIME, is suppressed: *Hora Prima supprimatur (89.e).*

PSALMS, to be redistributed: *Ut cursus Horarum, in art.
89 propositus, reapse observari possit, psalmi non amplius per unam hebdomadam, sed per longius temporis
spatium distribuantur (91).*

PSALTER, revision to be finished as soon as possible: *Opus recognitionis Psalterii feliciter inchoatum, quamprimum perducatur ad finem (91).*

PUBLIC WORSHIP, of the Church: *Officium divinum utpote oratio publica Ecclesiae (90).*

READING OF LIVES OF SAINTS IN, to accord with the facts of history: *Passiones seu vitae Sanctorum fidei historicae reddantur (92.c).*

READINGS OF THE FATHERS IN, to be better selected: *lectiones de operibus Patrum, Doctorum et Scriptorum ecclesiasticorum depromendae melius seligantur (92.b).*

REGULARS BOUND BY LAW OR CONSTITUTIONS, have the obligation to recite the entire office in choir: *totum Officium . . . Regularium ex iure vel constitutionibus choro adstrictorum (95.a).*

SCRIPTURE READINGS IN, shall be rearranged: *Lectio sacrae Scripturae ita ordinetur, ut thesauri verbi divini in pleniore amplitudine expedite adiri possint (92.a).*

SEQUENCE OF HOURS, to be restored so that they may be genuinely related to the time of the day when they are prayed, as far as this may be possible: *cursus Horarum traditus ita instauretur ut Horis veritas temporis, quantum fieri potest (88).*

SUBSTITUTED BY A LITURGICAL SERVICE, in appropriate instances to be defined by the rubrics: *Opportunae commutationes divini Officii cum actione liturgica a rubricis definiantur (97).*

SUNDAY VESPERS, to be restored in the parish: *Curent animarum pastores ut Horae praecipuae praesertim Vesperis, diebus dominicis et festis sollemnioribus, in ecclesia communiter celebrentur (100).*

TREASURES OF, to be so adapted that all those to whom they are handed on may more extensively and easily draw profit from them: *In instauratione vero peragenda, venerabilis ille romani Officii saecularis thesaurus ita aptetur, ut latius et facilius eo frui possint omnes quibus traditur (90).*

VERNACULAR IN CHORAL RECITATION, may be granted by the competent superior to nuns and to members of institutes dedicated to acquiring perfection, both men who are not clerics and women: *Monialibus, necnon sodalibus, sive viris non clericis sive mulieribus, Institutorum statuum perfectionis, in Officio divino, etiam in choro celebrando, concedi potest a Superiore competente ut lingua vernacula utantur (101:2).*

VERNACULAR IN PRIVATE RECITATION, may be granted by the ordinary in individual cases to those clerics for whom the use of Latin constitutes a grave obstacle to their praying properly: *facta tamen Ordinario potestate usum versionis vernaculae ad normam art. 36 confectae concedendi singulis pro casibus, iis clericis, quibus usus linguae latinae grave impedimentum est quominus Officium debite persolvant (101:1).*

VERNACULAR TRANSLATIONS, must be approved: *dummodo versio approbata sit (101:2).*

VOICE OF THE BRIDE, when performed by priests and others deputed, or by the faithful praying together with the priest in the approved form; then it is truly the voice of the bride addressed to her bridegroom: *Cum vero mirabile illud laudis canticum rite peragunt sacerdotes aliique ad hanc rem Ecclesiae instituto deputati vel christifideles una cum sacerdote forma probata orantes, tunc vere vox est ipsius Sponsae (84).*

DIVINE WORSHIP, MUSICAL INSTRUMENTS IN, may be admitted with the knowledge and consent of the competent territorial authority: *Alia vero instrumenta, de iudicio et consensu auctoritatis territorialis competentis . . . in cultum divinum admittere licet (120).*

PIPE ORGAN IN, the classic instrument in the Latin Church: *Organum tubulatum in Ecclesia latina magno in honore habeatur (120).*

DOGMATIC THEOLOGY AND LITURGY IN SEMINARIES, to be integrated: *Curent insuper aliarum disci-*

plinarum magistri, imprimis theologiae dogmaticae . . .
ita, ex intrinsecis propii uniuscuiusque obiecti, mysterium Christi et historiam salutis excolere, ut exinde
earum connexio cum Liturgia et unitas sacerdotalis institutionis aperte clarescant (16).

DUTY OF BISHOPS. See BISHOPS, DUTIES AND RIGHTS OF. Also
BISHOPS, NATIONAL CONFERENCE OF.

DUTY OF CLERGY, TO PREACH, at those Masses which
are celebrated with the assistance of the people on Sundays and feasts of obligation; it should not be omitted except for a serious reason: *Homilia . . . ut pars ipsius liturgiae valde commendatur; quinimmo in Missis quae
diebus dominicis et festis de praecepto concurrente populo celebrantur, ne omittatur, nisi gravi de causa* (52).

DUTY OF LAITY, TO PARTICIPATE, in the mystery of
faith by a good understanding of the rites and prayers:
*Ecclesia sollicitas curas eo intendit . . . christifideles
huic fidei mysterio . . . per ritus et preces id bene intellegentes, sacram actionem conscie, pie et actuose participent* (48).

EASTER, DATE OF, could be stabilized in the Gregorian
Calendar provided that those whom it may concern give
their assent: *Sacrosanctum Concilium non obnititur quin
festum Paschatis certae dominicae in Calendaro Gregoriano assignetur, assentientibus iis quorum intersit* (Appendix 1).

ELEMENTS, DIVINE AND HUMAN, constitute the essence of
the Church: *verae Ecclesiae naturam, cuius proprium est
esse humanam simul ac divinam* (2).

EPISCOPAL CONSECRATION. See CONSECRATION OF BISHOP.

EPISTLE AND GOSPEL OF NUPTIAL MASS, to be
read at the beginning of marriage rite celebrated outside
of Mass: *Si vero Sacramentum Matrimonii sine Missa*

celebratur, *Epistola et Evangelium Missae pro sponsis legantur in initio ritus (78).*

EUCHARIST, COMMUNION, recommended as a form of participation: *Itaque Ecclesiae sollicitas curas eo intendit ne christifideles huic fidei mysterio tamquam extranei . . . sed pie et actuose participent . . . mensa Corporis Domini reficiantur (48).*

COMMUNION BY HOSTS CONSECRATED DURING SAME MASS, is strongly recommended as a more perfect form of participation: *Valde commendatur illa perfectior Missae participatio qua fideles post Communionem sacerdotis ex eodem Sacrificio Corpus Dominicum sumunt (55).*

COMMUNION UNDER BOTH SPECIES, may be granted when the bishops think fit, not only to clerics and religious but also to the laity, in cases to be determined by the Apostolic See, as, for instance, to the newly ordained in the Mass of ordination, to the newly professed in the Mass of profession, to the newly baptized in the Mass which follows baptism: *Communio sub utraque specie . . . in casibus ab Apostolica Sede definiendis, tum clericis et religiosis, tum laicis concedi potest, de iudicio Episcoporum, veluti ordinatis in Missa sacrae suae ordinationis, professis in Missa religiosae suae professionis, neophytis in Missa quae Baptismum subsequitur (55).*

INSTITUTION, at the Last Supper, on the night when He was betrayed: *Salvator noster, in Cena novissima, qua nocte tradebatur, Sacrificium Eucharisticum Corporis et Sanguinis instituit (47).*

MYSTERIES OF CHRIST PRESENT, which the Church has never failed to celebrate: *Numquam exinde omisit Ecclesia quin in unum conveniret ad paschale mysterium celebrandum . . . Eucharistiam celebrando in qua "mortis eius victoria et triumphus repraesentatur" (6).*

SACRIFICE AND SACRAMENT, was instituted by Christ at the Last Supper to perpetuate the sacrifice of the Cross, and to leave a sacrament of love, a sign of unity, a bond of charity: *Salvator noster, in Cena novissima . . . Sacrificium Eucharisticum Corporis et Sanguinis sui instituit, quo Sacrificium Crucis . . . perpetuaret . . . sacramentum pietatis, signum unitatis, vinculum caritatis . . . datur (47).*

THANKSGIVING, which the Church has never failed to celebrate: *Numquam exinde omisit Ecclesia quin in . . . . . . celebrandum . . . Eucharistiam celebrando . . . simul gratias agendo "Deo super inenarrabili dono." (6).*

EXERCISES OF PIETY. *See* DEVOTIONS, POPULAR.

EXPERIMENTS, LITURGICAL, will be permitted by the legitimate authority over a determined period of time, as the case requires, among certain groups suited for the purpose: *Ut autem aptatio cum necessaria circumspectione fiat, eidem auctoritati ecclesiasticae territoriali ab Apostolica Sede facultas tribuetur, si casus ferat, ut in quibusdam coetibus ad id aptis et per determinatum tempus necessaria praevia experimenta permittat et dirigat (40.2).*

EXTREME UNCTION. *See* ANOINTING OF THE SICK.

EXTERNAL ELEMENTS IN LITURGY, subject to change: *Liturgia constat . . . partibus mutationi obnoxiis, quae decursu temporum variare possunt vel etiam debent (21).*

FAITHFUL, ACTIVE PARTICIPATION OF, in liturgical celebrations is earnestly desired by Mother Church: *Valde cupit Mater Ecclesia ut fideles universi ad plenam illam, consciam atque actuosam liturgicarum celebrationum participationem ducantur (14).*

is their right and duty by reason of their baptism: *Vi Baptismatis ius habet et officium (14).*

CHRISTIAN SPIRIT OF, is derived from the liturgy: *sacra Liturgia . . . est enim primus, isque necessarius fons, e quo spiritum vere christianum fideles hauriant (14).*

DIVINE OFFICE AND, they too are encouraged to recite it either with the priests, or among themselves, or even individually: *Commendatur ut et ipsi laici recitent Officium divinum, vel cum sacerdotibus, vel inter se congregati, quin immo unusquisque solus (100)*.

FORMATION OF, is completed in the various seasons of the year by means of pious practices for soul and body, by instruction, prayer, and works of penance and of mercy: *Variis denique anni temporibus iuxta traditas disciplinas, Ecclesia fidelium eruditionem perficit, per pias animi et corporis exercitationes, instructionem, precationem, paenitentiae et misericordiae opera (105)*.

INTELLIGENT PARTICIPATION OF, in Mass is earnestly desired by the Church. When present they should not be there as silent spectators or strangers; on the contrary, through a good understanding of the rites and prayers they should take their part in the sacred action, conscious of what they are doing, with devotion and full collaboration: *Itaque Ecclesia sollicitas curas eo intendit ne christifideles huic fidei mysterio tamquam extranei vel muti spectatores intersint, sed per ritus et preces id bene intellegentes, sacram actionem conscie, pie et actuose participent (48)*.

LITURGICAL INSTRUCTION OF, to be promoted by pastors with zeal and patience: *Liturgicam institutionem necnon actuosam fidelium participationem . . . animarum pastores sedulo ac patienter prosequantur (19)*.

PRIESTS AND, to be united in living and sharing the liturgical life: *Sacerdotes . . . vitam liturgicam vivant, eamque cum fidelibus sibi commissis communicent (18)*.

PROPER DISPOSITIONS OF, necessary so that the liturgy may be able to produce its full effects: *Ut haec tamen plena efficacitas habeatur, necessarium est ut fideles cum recti animi dispositionibus ad sacram Liturgiam accedant (11)*.

SACRAMENTAL SIGNS AND, their understanding is of the highest importance: *Maxime proinde interest ut fideles signa Sacramentorum facile intellegant (59).*

SHORTER BAPTISMAL RITE AND, to be drawn up for their use when there is danger of death, and neither priest nor deacon is available: *Conficiatur item Ordo brevior (Baptismi) quo . . . in periculo mortis, fideles, absente sacerdote vel diacono, uti possint (68).*

SUNDAY VESPERS AND, to be promoted by pastors: *Curent animarum pastores ut Horae praecipuae, praesertim Vesperae diebus dominicis et festis sollemnioribus, in ecclesia communiter celebrentur (100).*

VOCATION OF, to be the light of the world and to glorify their Father before men: *quibus operibus manifestum fiat christifideles de hoc mundo quidem non esse, sed tamen esse lucem mundi eosdemque Patrem glorificare coram hominibus (9).*

FAST, PASCHAL, to be observed everywhere on Good Friday, and where possible, prolonged throughout Holy Saturday: *sacrum tamen esto ieiunium paschale, feria VI in Passione et Morte Domini ubique celebrandum et, iuxta opportunitatem, etiam Sabbato sancto producendum (110).*

FEAST DAYS, VIGIL OF, bible services should be encouraged especially on the more solemn occasions: *foveatur sacra Verbi Dei celebratio in solemniorum festorum pervigiliis (35.4).*

FEASTS, BLESSED VIRGIN, occupy a place of special prominence in the liturgical year: *In hoc annuo mysteriorum Christi circulo celebrando, Sancta Ecclesia Beatam Mariam Dei Genetricem cum peculiari amore veneratur (103).*

MYSTERIES OF CHRIST'S LIFE, occupy a place of primacy in the liturgical year: *dies festos Domini, quibus mysteria salutis per annum celebrantur . . . Proinde Proprium de Tempore aptum suum locum obtineat super festa Sanctorum (108).*

SAINTS AND MARTYRS, occupy a place in the liturgical year: *Memorias insuper Martyrum aliorumque Sanctorum, circulo anni inseruit Ecclesia (104).*

shall be limited to a particular Church or nation or family of religious lest they take precedence over the feasts of the Lord: *Ne festa Sanctorum festis ipsa mysteria salutis recolentibus praevaleant, plura ex his particulari cuique Ecclesiae vel Nationi vel Religiosae Familiae relinquantur celebranda (111).*

to be extended to the universal Church only when they are of a truly universal importance: *iis tantum ad Ecclesiam universam extensis, quae Sanctos memorant momentum universale revera prae se ferentes (111).*

SUNDAY, the Church celebrates the paschal mystery: *Mysterium paschale Ecclesia, . . . octava quaque die celebrat (106).*

on this day the faithful should come together to celebrate the Eucharist: *Hac enim die christideles in unum convenire debent ut . . . Eucharistiam participantes (106).*

shall have precedence over all other celebrations unless they are truly of greatest importance: *dies dominica est primordialis dies festus . . . Aliae celebrationes, nisi revera sint maximi momenti, ipsi ne praeponantur (106).*

FLEXIBILITY IN THE LITURGY. See ADAPTATION.

FRIDAY, GOOD, paschal fast to be observed everywhere: *Sacrum tamen esto ieiunium paschale, feria VI in Passione et Morte Domini ubique celebrandum (110).*

FURNISHINGS, SACRED, ADAPTATIONS. ALL STYLES OF, are admitted according to the progress of the technical arts: *Sacra suppellex . . . eas mutationes sive in materia, sive in forma, sive in ornatu admittens, quas artis technicae progressus per temporis decursum invexit (122).*

ADAPTATIONS OF, especially with regard to the materials and form can be undertaken by the territorial bodies of bishops: *Qua in re, praesertim quoad materiam et formam sacrae suppellectilis et indumentorum, territorialibus Episcoporum facultas tribuitur res aptandi necessitatibus et moribus locorum, ad normam art. 22 huius Constitutionis (128).*

ORDINARIES AND, must be very careful to see that works of value are not disposed of or dispersed: *Sedulo advigilent Ordinarii ne sacra supellex vel opera pretiosa, utope ornamenta domus Dei, alienentur vel disperdantur (126).*

GESTURES, BODILY, BY MEANS OF, active participation is promoted: *Ad actuosam participationem promovendam, populi . . . actiones seu gestus et corporis foveantur (30).*

GOOD FRIDAY. See FRIDAY, GOOD.

GOSPEL AND HOMILY, MARRIAGE CEREMONY AFTER, and before the "prayer of the faithful" when matrimony is celebrated within Mass: *Matrimonium ex more intra Missam celebretur, post lectionem Evangelii et homiliam, ante "orationem fidelium" (78).*

GREGORIAN CHANT. See MUSIC.

HIERARCHY. See BISHOP; BISHOPS, DUTIES AND RIGHTS OF; BISHOPS, NATIONAL CONFERENCE OF.

HOLY DAYS, THE COMMON PRAYER IN MASS, to be restored: *"Oratio communis" seu "fidelium" post Evangelium et homiliam, praesertim diebus dominicis et festis de praecepto (53).*

SERMON AND, not to be omitted except for a serious reason: *Homilia . . . quinimmo in Missis quae diebus* dominicis et festis de praecepto concurrente populo celebrantur, ne omittatur, nisi gravi de causa (52).

VESPERS AND, to be celebrated in common in church: Curent animarum pastores ut Horae praecipuae, praesertim Vesperae, diebus dominicis et festis sollemnioribus, in ecclesia communiter celebrentur (100).

HOLY THURSDAY, CONCELEBRATION, permitted not only at the Mass of the Chrism, but also at the evening Mass: facultatem concelebrandi ad sequentes casus Concilio extendere feria V in Cena Domini, tum ad Missam chrismatis, tum ad Missam vespertinam (57:1.1a).

HOMILY. See PREACHING.

HONORS TO CIVIL AUTHORITIES, are provided for in the liturgy: In Liturgia . . . honores ad normam legum liturgicarum auctoritatibus civilibus debitos (32).

PROHIBITED, in the liturgy, to any private persons or classes of persons whether in the ceremonies or by external display: honores . . . nulla privatarum personarum aut condicionum, sive in caerimoniis, sive in exterioribus pompis, habeatur acceptio (32).

HYMNS AND PSALMS, BY MEANS OF, active participation is promoted: Ad actuosam participationem promovendam, populi . . . psalmodia, antiphonae, cantica . . . foveantur (29).

IMAGES, ARRANGEMENT OF, their relative positions in churches should reflect right order: in ecclesiis sacris imagines . . . congruo ordine exponantur (125).

IN CHURCH, custom to be retained: Firma maneat praxis, in ecclesiis sacras imagines fidelium venerationi proponendi (125).

LAWS REGARDING, to be revised. This refers especially to their proper ordering: Canones et statuta ecclesiastica quae rerum externarum ad sacrum cultum . . . spec-

tant . . . praesertim . . . *congruentem sacrarum
imaginum . . . quam primum recognoscantur (128).*
NUMBER OF, to be limited: *moderato numero (125).*

INDIVIDUAL CHURCHES, DEVOTIONS PROPER TO, enjoy a special dignity if they are undertaken by mandate
of the bishops according to customs or books lawfully
approved: *Speciali quoque dignitate gaudent sacra Ecclesiarum particularium exercitia, quae de mandato Episcoporum celebrantur, secundum consuetudines aut libros
legitime approbatos (13).*

INDIVIDUAL MASSES, THE RIGHT OF PRIEST TO CELE-
BRATE, is retained though not at the same time in the
same church as a concelebrated Mass, nor on Thursday
of the Lord's Supper: *Salva tamen semper sit cuique
sacerdoti facultas Missam singularem celebrandi, non vero
eodem tempore in eadem ecclesia, nec feria V in Cena
Domini (57:2.2).*

INFANT BAPTISM. See BAPTISM, INFANTS.

INITIATION RITES, IN MISSION LANDS, elements from
these, when capable of being adapted to Christian ritual,
may be admitted along with those already found in Christian tradition, according to the norm laid down in Art.
37–40 of this Constitution: *In terris Missionum, praeter
ea quae in traditione christiana habentur, illa etiam elementa initiationis admitti liceat, quae apud unumquemque populum in usu esse reperiuntur, quatenus ritui christiano accommodari possunt, ad normam art. 37–40 huius
Constitutionis (65).*

INNOVATIONS, IN LITURGY, are curbed by the Church:
*Quapropter nemo omnino alius, etiamsi sit sacerdos,
quidquam proprio marte in Liturgia addat, demat, aut
mutet (22:3).*

are forbidden unless the good of the Church genuinely
and certainly requires them: *Innovationes, demum,
ne fiant nisi vera et certa utilitas Ecclesiae id exigat
(23).*

INSTITUTE FOR PASTORAL LITURGY, to assist the Liturgical Commission established by the competent territorial ecclesiastical authority mentioned in Art. 22:2: *A competenti auctoritate ecclesiastica territoriali, de qua in art. 22:2, expedit ut instituatur Commissio liturgica . . . Cui Commissioni, in quantum fieri potest, opem ferat quoddam Institutum Liturgiae Pastoralis (44).*

INSTRUCTION, LITURGICAL, IN SEMINARIES, to be ranked among the compulsory and major courses. In theological faculties it is to rank among the principal courses: *Disciplina de sacra Liturgia in seminariis et studiorum domibus religiosis inter disciplinas necessarias et potiores, in facultatibus autem theologicis inter disciplinas principales est habenda (16).*

PASTORS TO GIVE, so that full and active participation of the people may be restored to them: *Quae totius . . . et actuosa participatio, in instauranda et fovenda sacra Liturgia . . . et ideo in tota actione pastorali per debitam instructionem, ab animarum pastoribus est sedulo adpetenda (14).*

PRIESTS' NEED OF, so that they might understand ever more fully what it is that they are doing when they perform the sacred rites: *Sacerdotes, sive saeculares sive religiosi, in vinea Domini iam operantes, omnibus mediis opportunis iuventur ut plenius semper quae in functionibus sacris agunt intellegant (18).*

SHOULD BE GIVEN in a variety of ways; if necessary, short directives to be spoken by the priest or proper minister should be provided within the rites themselves. But they should occur only at the more suitable moments, and be in prescribed or similar words: *Etiam catechesis directius liturgica omnibus modis inculcetur; et in ipsis ritibus si necessariae sint, breves admonitiones, a sacerdote vel competenti ministro, opportunioribus tantum momentis, praescriptis vel similibus verbis, dicendae, praevideantur (35.3).*

INSTRUMENTAL MUSIC, PIPE ORGAN, is the Latin Church's classical instrument: *Organum tubulatum in Ecclesia latina magno in honore habeatur (120)*.

> VARIOUS KINDS OF, may also be admitted for use in divine worship, with the knowledge and consent of the competent territorial authority, as laid down in Art. 22:2, 37 and 40. This may be done, however, only on condition that the instruments are suitable, or can be made suitable for sacred use, accord with the dignity of the temple, and truly contribute to the edification of the faithful: *Alia vero instrumenta, de iudicio et consensu auctoritatis territorialis competentis, ad normam art. 22:2, 37 et 40, in cultum divinum admittere licet, quatenus usui sacro apta sint aut aptari possint, templi dignitati congruant, atque revera aedificationi fidelium faveant (120)*.

INTERCESSORY PRAYERS, IN MASS, to be restored, after the Gospel and the homily, especially on Sundays and feasts of obligation: *"Oratio communis" seu "fidelium" post Evangelium et homiliam, praesertim diebus dominicis et festis de praecepto, restituatur (53)*.

LAITY, TO ADMINISTER SACRAMENTALS, at least in special circumstances and at the discretion of the ordinary. *Provideatur ut quaedam Sacramentalia, saltem in specialibus rerum adiunctis et de iudicio Ordinarii, a laicis congruis qualitatibus praeditis administrari possint (79)*.

> BAPTISMAL EFFECTS AND, they receive the spirit of adoption as sons "in which we cry: Abba, Father": *per Baptismum homines . . . spiritum accipiunt adoptionis filiorum, "in quo clamamus: Abba Pater" (6)*.

> AS CHOIR SINGERS, perform a genuine liturgical function: *ii qui ad scholam cantorum pertinent, vero ministerio liturgico funguntur (29)*.

AS COMMENTATORS, perform a genuine liturgical function: *commentatores . . . vero ministerio liturgico funguntur (29).*

DIVINE OFFICE AND, encouraged to recite either with the priests, or among themselves, or even individually: *Commendatur ut et ipsi laici recitent Officium divinum, vel cum sacerdotibus, vel inter se congregati, quin immo unusquisque solus (100).*

it is public worship when they pray together with the priest in the approved form: *Cum vero mirabile illud laudis canticum . . . christifideles una cum sacerdote forma probata orantes, tunc vere vox est ipsius Sponsae (84).*

AS LECTORS, perform a genuine liturgical function: *lectores . . . vero ministerio liturgico funguntur (29).*

PARTICIPATION IN LITURGY OF, to be promoted by pastors: *Liturgicam institutionem necnon actuosam fidelium participationem . . . animarum pastores sedulo ac patienter prosequantur (19).*

is the earnest desire of the Church: *Valde cupit Mater Ecclesia ut fideles universi ad plenam illam, consciam atque actuosam liturgicarum celebrationum participationem ducantur (14).*

promoted by acclamations, responses, psalmody, antiphons, and songs, as well as by actions, gestures and bodily attitudes: *ad actuosam participationem promovendam populi acclamationes, responsiones, psalmodia, antiphonae, cantica, necnon actiones seu gestus et corporis habitus foveantur (30).*

is their right and duty by reason of baptism: *participationem ducantur . . . vi Baptismatis ius habet et officium (14).*

PASTORAL INSTITUTE OF LITURGY AND, to assist the liturgical Commission set up by the competent ecclesiastical authority, consisting of experts in these matters: *A competenti auctoritate ecclesiastica territoriali . . . instituantur Commissio liturgica, a viris . . . peritis* iuvanda . . . *in quantum fieri potest, opem ferat quoddam Institutum Liturgiae Pastoralis, constans sodalibus, non exclusis, si res ita ferat, laicis in hac materia praestantibus (44).*

AS SERVORS, perform a genuine liturgical function: *etiam ministrantes . . . vero ministerio liturgico funguntur (29).*

LANGUAGE. See VERNACULAR.

LATIN IN DIVINE OFFICE, to be retained by clerics: *Iuxta saecularem traditionem ritus latini, in Officio divino lingua latina clericis servanda est (101:1).*

IN THE LATIN RITES, is to be preserved, particular law remaining in force: *Linguae latinae usus, salvo particulari iure, in Ritibus latinis servetur (36:1).*

ORDINARY OF THE MASS AND FAITHFUL, steps should be taken so that they may also be able to say or sing together those parts which pertain to them: *Provideatur tamen ut christifideles etiam lingua latina partes Ordinarii Missae quae ad ipsos spectant possint simul dicere vel cantare (54).*

LAUDS, CHARACTER OF, a morning prayer: *Laudes, ut preces matutinae (89.a).*

LAYING ON OF HANDS, EPISCOPAL CONSECRATION AND, may be done by all bishops present: *In Consecratione Episcopali impositionem manuum fieri licet ab omnibus Episcopis praesentibus (76).*

LECTORS IN THE LITURGY, exercise a genuine liturgical function: *lectores . . . vero ministerio liturgico funguntur (29).*

LENT, ADAPTATION OF PENITENTIAL PRACTICES, in ways that are possible in our own times and in different regions, and according to the circumstances of the faithful: *Praxis vero paenitentialis, iuxta nostra aetatis et diversarum regionum possibilitates necnon fidelium condiciones, foveatur (110).*

BAPTISMAL FEATURES OF, more use is to be made: *elementa baptismalia liturgiae quadragesimalis propria abundatius adhibeantur (19.a)*.

BAPTISMAL FEATURES OF FORMER TIMES, to be restored as may seem good: *quaedam vero ex anteriore traditione, pro opportunitate, restituantur (109.a)*.

BIBLE SERVICES IN, to be encouraged: *Foveatur sacra Verbi Dei celebratio . . . in aliquibus feriis . . . Quadragesimae (35.4)*.

INSTRUCTION DURING, to impress on the minds of the faithful not only the social consequences of sin but also that the true essence of penance consists in a detestation of sin because it is an offense against God: *Quoad catechesim autem animis fidelium inculcetur, una cum consectariis socialibus peccati, illa propria paenitentiae natura quae peccatum, prout est offensa Dei detestatur (109.b)*.

PENITENTIAL ELEMENTS, more use is to be made in the liturgy: *elementa paenitentialia (liturgiae quadragesimalis propria) abundatius adhibeantur (109.b)*.

PENITENTIAL PRACTICES, NATURE OF, should not only be internal and individual, but also external and social: *Paenitentia temporis quadragesimalis non tantum sit interna et individualis, sed quoque externa et socialis (110)*.

TWOFOLD CHARACTER OF, to primarily recall or prepare for baptism, and to perform penance: *Duplex indoles temporis quadragesimalis, quod praesertim per memoriam vel preparationem Baptismi et per paenitentiam (109)*.

LITTLE OFFICE, NATURE OF, a genuine liturgical function when recited by those, in virtue of their Constitution, provided that it is drawn up after the pattern of the Divine Office and is duly approved: *Item, publicam Ecclesiae orationem agunt, si quod parvum Officium, vi Constitutionum recitant, dummodo in modum Officii divini confectum ac rite approbatum sit (98)*.

LITURGICAL APOSTOLATE, COMPETENT TERRITORIAL
ECCLESIASTICAL AUTHORITY AND, to promote and direct
by establishing a Commission for the liturgy: *A competenti auctoritate ecclesiastica territoriali . . . expedit
ut instituatur Commissio liturgica . . . a viris . . .
peritis iuvanda . . . Ipsius Commissionis erit, ductu
auctoritatis ecclesiasticae territorialis . . . actionem pastoralem liturgicam . . . moderari . . . (44).*

PASTORS AND, to zealously strive to achieve active participation of the faithful: *Totius populi plena et actuosa
participatio . . . et ideo in tota actione pastorali
. . . ab animarum pastoribus est sedulo adpetenda
(14).*

ZEAL FOR PROMOTION OF, a sign of the providential dis-
position of God in our time: *Sacrae Liturgiae fovendae
atque instaurandae studium merito habetur veluti
signum providentialium dispositionum Dei super nostra
aetate (43).*

LITURGICAL BOOKS, ADAPTATIONS IN, to be provided
according to different groups, regions, and peoples, especially in mission lands: *Servata substantiali unitate ritus
romani, legitimis varietatibus et aptationibus ad diversos
coetus, regiones, populos, praesertim in Missionibus, locus
relinquatur, etiam cum libri liturgici recognoscuntur (38).*

TO BE REVISED, as soon as possible: *Libri liturgici quam
primum recognoscantur (25).*

RUBRICS AND, provision to be made also for people's parts
in the revision: *In libris liturgicis recognoscendis,
sedulo attendatur ut rubricae etiam partes fidelium
praevideant (31).*

LITURGICAL CELEBRATIONS, ACTIVE PARTICIPATION
IN, is the preeminent manifestation of the Church: *sibi
persuasum habentes praecipuam manifestationem Ecclesiae haberi in plenaria et actuosa participatione totius
plebis sanctae Dei in iisdem celebrationibus liturgicis
(41).*

CHOIR MEMBERS IN, perform a genuine liturgical function: *(in celebrationes liturgicis)* . . . *ii qui ad scholam cantorum pertinent, vero ministerio liturgico funguntur (29).*

COMMENTATORS IN, perform a genuine liturgical function: *commentatores . . . vero ministerio liturgico funguntur (29).*

DIFFERENT ROLES FOR DIFFERENT MEMBERS IN, each to perform all, or only those parts which pertain to his office by the nature of the rite and the principles of liturgy: *In celebrationibus liturgicis quisque, sive minister sive fidelis, munere suo fungens, solum et totum id agat, quod ad ipsum ex rei natura et normis liturgicis pertinet (28).*

LECTORS IN, perform a genuine liturgical function: *lectores . . . vero ministerio liturgico funguntur (29).*

SERVERS IN, perform a genuine liturgical function: *ministrantes . . . vero ministerio liturgico funguntur (29).*

LITURGICAL COMMISSION, DIOCESE AND, to be established under the direction of the bishop to promote the liturgical apostolate: *in singulis dioecesibus Commissio de sacra Liturgica habeatur, ad actionem liturgicam, moderante Episcopo, promovendam (45).*

COMPETENT TERRITORIAL ECCLESIASTICAL AUTHORITY AND, to be established and assisted by experts: *A competenti auctoritate ecclesiastica territoriali . . . expedit ut instituatur Commissio liturgica, a viris . . . peritis iuvanda (44).*

LITURGICAL EXPERIMENTS, are allowed as the case requires: *Ut autem aptatio cum necessaria circumspectione fiat . . . si casus ferat . . . per determinatum tempus necessaria praevia experimenta permittat (40.2).*

REGULATION OF, the Apostolic See will grant power to the territorial ecclesiastical authority to permit and direct: *eidem auctoritati ecclesiasticae territoriali ab Apostolica*

*Sede facultas tribuetur, si casus ferat, . . . experi-
menta permittat et dirigat (40.2).*

LITURGICAL FORMATION IN SEMINARIES, neces-
sary for the spiritual life of clerics: *Clerici, in seminariis
domibusque religiosis, formationem vitae spiritualis liturgicam acquirant (16).*

LITURGICAL FUNCTIONS, NATURE OF, they are celebrations of the Church, the entire body of the Church:
*Actiones liturgicae non sunt actiones privatae, sed cele-
brationes Ecclesiae . . . Quare ad universum Corpus
Ecclesiae pertinent (26).*

LITURGICAL INNOVATIONS, prohibited by any person, even if he be a priest: *nemo omnino alius, etiamsi sit
sacerdos, quidquam proprio marte in Liturgia addat, demat, aut mutet (22:3).*

LITURGICAL INSTRUCTION, OF CLERGY, they are to
to be helped by every suitable means to understand ever
more fully what it is they are doing when they perform
the sacred rites: *Sacerdotes, sive saeculares sive religiosi, in
vinea Domini iam operantes, omnibus mediis opportunis
iuventur ut plenius semper quae in functionibus sacris
agunt intellegant (18).*

OF FAITHFUL, must be promoted by pastors: *Liturgicam
institutionem . . . animarum pastores sedulo ac patienter prosequantur (19).*

pastors must strive to achieve active participation by
means of the necessary instruction: *et ideo in tota
actione pastorali, per debitam institutionem, ab animarum pastoribus est sedulo adpetenda (14).*

IN SEMINARIES, clerics will need proper direction, so that
they may be able to understand the sacred rites and
take part in them whole-heartedly: *Clerici, in seminariis domibusque religiosis . . . cum apta manuduc-
tione qua sacros ritus intellegere et toto animo participare queant (17).*

WITHIN THE RITES, to be given in a variety of ways: *Cate-chesis directus liturgica omnibus modis inculcetur; et in ipsis ritibus, si necessariae sint, breves admonitiones, a sacerdote vel competenti ministro (35.3).*

LITURGICAL LAWS, ADAPTATIONS AND, because they often involve special difficulties, particularly in mission lands, men who are experts in these matters must be employed to formulate them: *Quia leges liturgicae difficultates speciales, quoad aptationem, praesertim in Missionibus, secum ferre solent, in illis condendis praesto sint viri, in re de qua agitur, periti (40.3).*

ON MATERIAL THINGS IN WORSHIP, to be revised: *Canones et statuta ecclesiastica, quae rerum externarum ad sacrum cultum pertinentium apparatum spectant . . . . . . quam primum recognoscantur (128).*

LITURGICAL LIFE, PARISH AND, must be fostered theoretically and practically among the faithful and clergy in its relationship to the bishop: *vita liturgica paroeciae eiusque relatio ad Episcopum in mente et praxi fidelium et cleri fovenda est (42).*

LITURGICAL READINGS IN DIVINE OFFICE, to be better selected: *lectiones de operibus Patrum, Doctorum et Scriptorum ecclesiasticorum depromendae melius seligantur (92.b).*

LITURGICAL REGULATION, THE RIGHT OF, depends solely on the authority of the Church, that is, on the Apostolic See and, as laws may determine, on the bishop: *Sacre Liturgiae moderatio ab Ecclesiae auctoritate unice pendet: quae quidem est apud Apostolicam Sedem et, normam iuris, apud Episcopum (22:1).*

COMPETENT TERRITORIAL BODIES OF BISHOPS AND, depends also on them within certain defined limits in virtue of power conceded by law: *ex potestate a iure concessa, rei liturgicae moderatio inter limites statutos pertinet quoque ad competentes varii generis terri-*

toriales *Episcoporum coetus legitime constitutos* *(22:2)*.

LITURGICAL RESTORATION, ᴀɪᴍ ᴏғ, that the Christian people may more certainly derive an abundance of graces: *Pia Mater Ecclesia, ut populus christianus in sacra Liturgia abundantim gratiarum securius assequatur, ipsius Liturgiae instaurationem sedulo curare cupit (21).*

LITURGICAL SCIENCE, ᴇxᴘᴇʀᴛs ᴏғ, to assist the liturgical Commission established by the competent territorial ecclesiastical authority: *A competenti auctoritate ecclesiastica territoriali, de qua in art. 22:2, expedit ut instituatur Commissio liturgica, a viris in scientia liturgica . . . peritis iuvanda (44).*

LITURGICAL SERVICES, ᴄᴏɴɢʀᴇɢᴀᴛɪᴏɴᴀʟ sɪɴɢɪɴɢ ɪɴ, to be skilfully fostered: *Cantus popularis religiosus sollerter foveatur, ita ut in piis sacrisque exercitiis et in ipsis liturgicis actionibus iuxta normas et praecepta rubricarum, fidelium voces resonare possint (118).*

ᴅɪᴠɪɴᴇ ᴏғғɪᴄᴇ ᴀɴᴅ, appropriate instances are to be defined by the rubrics in which there may be a substitution for the Divine Office: *Opportunae commutationes divini Officii cum actione liturgica a rubricis definiantur (97).*

LITURGICAL TEXTS, ʀᴇsᴛᴏʀᴀᴛɪᴏɴ ᴀɴᴅ, to be drawn up so that they more clearly express the holy things which they signify: *Qua quidem instauratione, textus . . . ita ordinari oportet, ut sancta, quae significant, clarius exprimant (21).*

ʟɪᴛᴜʀɢɪᴄᴀʟ ʏᴇᴀʀ. See ʏᴇᴀʀ, ʟɪᴛᴜʀɢɪᴄᴀʟ.

LITURGY, ᴀᴄᴛɪᴏɴ ᴏғ ᴛʜᴇ ᴍʏsᴛɪᴄᴀʟ ʙᴏᴅʏ, the whole public worship is performed by the head and his members: *omnis liturgica celebratio . . . opus Christi sacerdotis, eiusque Corporis, quod est Ecclesia (7).*

ᴀᴅᴀᴘᴛᴀᴛɪᴏɴ, admitted according to the genius and talents of the various races and peoples: *Ecclesia, in iis quae fidem aut bonum totius communitatis non tangunt*

. . . quinimmo, variarum gentium populorumque animi ornamenta ac dotes colit et provehit . . . quandoque in ipsam Liturgiam admittit (37).

ADAPTATION OF NATIVE INITIATION RITES, may be admitted in the Christian ritual along with those already found in Christian tradition: In terris Missionum, praeter ea quae in traditione christiana habentur, illa elementa initiationis admitti liceat, quae apud unumquemque populum in usu esse reperiuntur, quatenus ritui christiano accommodari possunt (65).

ADAPTATION OF NATIVE MUSIC, in certain parts of the world, especially in mission lands, may be admitted: Cum in regionibus quibusdam, praesertim Missionum, gentes inveniantur quibus propria est traditio musica . . . quam in cultu ad earum indolem accommodando (119).

AIM OF RESTORATION, that the Christian may more certainly derive an abundance of graces: Pia Mater Ecclesia, ut populus christianus in sacra Liturgia abundantiam gratiarum securius assequatur, ipsius Liturgiae generalem instaurationem sedulo curare cupit (21).

CHANGES TO BE INVESTIGATED, into each part that is to be revised, so that sound tradition may be retained, and yet the way remain open to legitimate progress: Ut sana traditio retineatur et tamen via legitimae progressioni aperiatur, de singulis partibus recognoscendis accurata investigatio theologica, historica, pastoralis semper praecedat (23).

CHRIST ALWAYS PRESENT IN, He is present in the sacrifice of the Mass . . . especially under the eucharistic species. By His power He is present in the Sacraments . . . He is present in His word . . . He is present, lastly, when the Church prays and sings: Ad tantum vero opus perficiendum, Christus Ecclesiae suae semper adest, praesertim in actionibus liturgicis. Praesens adest in Missae Sacrificio . . . maxime sub speciebus eucharisticis. Praesens adest virtute sua in Sacramentis

. . . praesens adest in verbo suo . . . praesens adest
denique dum supplicat et psallit Ecclesia (7).

CHRIST'S REDEMPTIVE WORK IN, is accomplished, most of
all in the divine sacrifice of the eucharist: *Liturgia
enim, per quam, maxime in divino Eucharistiae Sacrificio, "opus nostrae Redemptionis exercetur" (2).*

CHURCH'S ACTIVITY NOT EXHAUSTED IN, before men come
to it they must be called to faith and conversion: *Sacra
Liturgia non explet totam actionem Ecclesiae; nam
antequam homines ad Liturgiam accedere possint,
necesse est ut ad fidem et conversionem vocentur (9).*

COMPETENT TERRITORIAL ECCLESIASTICAL AUTHORITY
AND ADAPTATIONS, to judge what elements from the
traditions and culture of individual peoples might be
appropriately admitted: *A competenti auctoritate ecclesiastica territoriali de qua in art 22:2, sedulo et prudenter consideretur quid, hoc in negotio, ex traditionibus ingenioque singulorum populorum opportune in
cultum divinum admitti possit (40.1).*

COMPETENT TERRITORIAL ECCLESIASTICAL AUTHORITY
AND COMMISSION FOR, to be established: *A competenti
auctoritate ecclesiastica territoriali, de qua in art. 22:2,
expedit ut instituantur Commissio liturgica, de viris in
scientia liturgica, Musica, Arte sacra ac re pastorali
peritis iuvanda (44).*

DIDACTIC ROLE OF, though it is above all things the worship of the divine Majesty, it likewise contains much
instruction for the faithful: *Etsi sacra Liturgia est
praecipue cultus divinae maiestatis, magnam etiam con-
tinet populi fidelis eruditionem (33).*

DIFFERENT ROLE FOR DIFFERENT PERSONS, and each
should do all of, but only, those parts which pertain
to his office by nature of the rite and the principles of
liturgy: *In celebrationibus liturgicis quisque, sive minister sive fidelis, munere suo fungens, solum et totum
id agat, quod ad ipsum ex rei natura et normis liturgicis pertinet (28).*

DIOCESAN COMMISSION FOR, to be established: *in singulis diocesibus Commissio de sacra Liturgia habeatur, ad actionem liturgicam, moderante Episcopo, promovendam (45)*.

DISTINCTIVE QUALITY OF, we take part in a foretaste of that heavenly liturgy which is celebrated in the holy city of Jerusalem, towards which we journey as pilgrims: *In terrena Liturgia caelestem illam praegustando participamus, quae in sancta civitate Ierusalem ad quam peregrini tendimus, celebratur (8)*.

DIVINE AND HUMAN ELEMENTS IN, are of its essence: *Liturgia constat parte immutabili, utpote divinitus instituta, et partibus mutationi obnoxiis (21)*.

DIVINE ELEMENTS IN, are immutable, being divinely instituted: *Liturgia constat parte immutabili, utpote divinitus instituta (21)*.

ECCLESIASTICAL REGULATION OF, depends solely on the authority of the Church, that is, on the Apostolic See and, as laws may determine, on the bishop: *Sacrae Liturgiae moderatio ab Ecclesiae auctoritate unice pendet: quae quidem est apud Apostolicam Sedem et, ad normam iuris, apud Episcopum (22:1)*.

In virtue of power conceded by the law, within certain defined limits it belongs also to the various kinds of competent territorial bodies of bishops legitimately established: *Ex potestate a iure concessa, rei liturgicae moderatio inter limites statutos pertinet quoque ad competentes varii generis territoriales Episcoporum coetus legitime constitutos (22:2)*.

EFFICACIOUS MEANS OF FULFILLING CHRISTIAN APOSTOLATE IN, it strengthens men's power to preach Christ, and thus shows forth the Church to those who are outside as a sign lifted up among the nations: *miro modo simul vires eorum ad praedicandum Christum roborat, et sic Ecclesiam iis qui sunt foris ostendit us signum levatum in nationes (2)*.

EFFICACIOUS SIGNS OF, are perceptible to the senses, and sanctification is effected in a way which corresponds with each of these: *in qua per signa sensibilia significatur et modo singulis proprio efficitur sanctificatio hominis (7)*.

EXPRESSION OF FAITH, it is the outstanding means whereby the faithful may express in their lives, and manifest to others, the mystery of Christ and the real nature of the true Church: *Liturgica enim . . . summe eo confert ut fideles vivendo exprimant et aliis manifestent mysterium Christi et genuinam verae Ecclesiae naturam (2)*.

FORMATION OF SEMINARIANS IN, necessary for their spiritual life: *Clerici, in seminariis domibusque religiosis, formationem vitae spiritualis liturgicam acquirant (17)*.

GLORY OF GOD AND SANCTIFICATION OF MEN, is achieved in the most efficacious possible way: *Ex Liturgia ergo, praecipue ex Eucharistia, ut e fonte, gratia in nos derivatur et maxima cum efficacia obtinetur illa in Christo hominum sanctificatio et Dei glorificatio (10)*.

HUMAN ELEMENTS IN, are subject to change. These not only may but ought to be changed with the passage of time if they have suffered from the intrusion of anything out of harmony with the inner nature of the liturgy or have become unsuited to it: *Nam Liturgia constat . . . partibus mutationi obnoxiis, quae decursu temporum variare possunt vel etiam debent, si in eas forte irrepserint quae minus bene ipsius Liturgiae intimae naturae respondeat, vel minus aptae factae sint (21)*.

IMPORTANCE IN THE SEMINARY, is to rank among the compulsory and major courses: *Disciplina de sacra Liturgia in seminariis et studiorum domibus religiosis inter disciplinas necessarias et potiores (16)*.

INNOVATIONS IN, forbidden unless the good of the Church genuinely and certainly requires them: *innovationes,* demum, ne fiant nisi vera et certa utilitas Ecclesiae id exigat (23).

forbidden to any person on his own authority, even if he be a priest: nemo omnino alius, etiamsi sit sacerdos, quidquam proprio marte in Liturgia addat, demat, aut mutet (22:3).

INTEGRATION IN THEOLOGICAL STUDIES, by professors of dogmatic, spiritual, and pastoral theology and holy Scripture. While striving to expound the mystery of salvation from the angle proper to each of their own subjects, they nevertheless must do so in a way which will clearly bring out the connection between their subject and liturgy, as also the unity that underlies all priestly training: Curent insuper aliarum disciplinarum (theologicarum) magistri, imprimis theologiae dogmaticae, sacrae Scripturae, theologiae spiritualis et pastoralis ita, ex intrinsecis exigentiis proprii uniuscuiusque obiecti, mysterium Christi et historiam salutis excolere, ut exinde earum connexio cum Liturgia et unitas sacerdotalis institutionis aperte clarescant (16).

IN THEOLOGICAL FACULTIES, to rank among the principal courses: in facultatibus autem theologicis inter disciplinas principales est habenda (16).

MINISTERS IN, exercise a genuine liturgical function: ministrantes . . . vero ministerio liturgico funguntur (29).

MYSTERY OF CHRIST ACTING IN, thus by baptism men are plunged into the paschal mystery of Christ: they die with Him, are buried with Him, and rise with Him; they receive the spirit of adoption as sons . . . in like manner as often as they eat the supper of the Lord they proclaim the death of the Lord until He comes: sic per Baptismum homines paschali Christi mysterio inseruntur: commortui, consepulti, conresuscitati; spiritum accipiunt adoptionis filiorum . . . Similiter quotiescumque dominicam cenam manducant, mortem Domini annuntiant donec veniat (6).

NATURE OF, Christ always associates the Church with Himself in this great work wherein God is perfectly glorified and men are sanctified. Rightly then the liturgy is considered as an exercise of the priestly office of Jesus Christ . . . in it the whole public worship is performed by the mystical body of Jesus Christ, that is, by the head and his members: *Reapse tanto in opere, quo Deus perfecte glorificatur, et homines sanctificantur, Christus Ecclesiam . . . sibi semper consociat . . . merito igitur Liturgia habetur veluti Iesu Christi sacerdotalis muneris exercitatio . . . a mystico Iesu Christi Corpore, Capite nempe eiusque membris, integer cultus publicus exercetur (7).*

NATURE OF INSTRUCTION IN SEMINARIES, to be taught under its theological, historical, spiritual, pastoral and juridical aspects: *sub aspectu cum theologico et historico, tum spirituali, pastorali et iuridico tradenda (16).*

PARTICIPATION IN, by acclamations, responses, psalmody, antiphons, and songs, as well as by actions, gestures, and bodily attitudes: *Ad actuosam participationem promovendam, populi acclamationes, responsiones, psalmodia, antiphonae, cantica, necnon actiones seu gestus et corporis habitus foveantur (30).*

by intelligent understanding of the rites and prayers: *christifideles huic fidei mysterio . . . per ritus et preces id bene intellegentes . . . pie et actuose participent (48).*

by listening to God's word: *verbo Dei instituantur (48).*

by offering the immaculate victim through and with the priest: *immaculatam hostiam, non tantum sacerdotis manus, sed etiam cum ipso offerentes, seipsos offerre discant (48).*

by proper dispositions: *Ut haec tamen plena efficacitas habeatur, necessarium est ut fideles cum recti animi dispositionibus ad sacram Liturgicam accedant (11).*

by receiving Communion consecrated during the same

Mass: *Valde commendatur illa perfectior Missae participatio qua fideles post Communionem sacerdotis ex eodem Sacrificio Corpus Dominicum sumunt* (55).

by singing together with the congregation: *in qualibet actione sacra in cantu peragenda universus fidelium coetus actuosam participationem sibi propriam praestare valeat, ad normam art. 28 et 30* (114).

is earnestly desired by Mother Church: *Valde cupit Mater Ecclesia ut fideles universi ad plenam illam, consciam atque actuosam liturgicarum celebrationum participationem ducantur* (14).

is demanded by its very nature: *actuosam . . . participationem . . . quae ab ipsius Liturgiae postulatur* (14).

is the right and duty of Christian people in virtue of their baptism: *ad quam populus christianus "genus electum regale sacerdotium, gens sancta, populus adquisitionis"* (1 Pet. 2:9; cf. 2:4–5), *vi Baptismatis ius habet et officium* (14).

pastors to promote by necessary instruction in all their pastoral work: *et ideo in tota actione pastorali (totius plena et actuosa participatio) per debitam institutionem, ab animarum pastoribus est sedulo adpetenda* (14). (cf. also 19.)

PRIESTLY OFFICE OF CHRIST, is continued: *Merito igitur Liturgia habetur veluti Iesu Christi sacerdotalis muneris exercitatio* (7).

AS PROFESSION OF FAITH, it prays that "they may hold fast in their lives to what they have grasped by their faith": *orat ut "vivendo teneant quod fide perceperunt"* (10).

REVERENCES TO CIVIL AUTHORITIES IN, are provided for: *In Liturgia . . . honores ad normam legum liturgicarum auctoritatibus civilibus debitos . . . habeatur acceptio* (32).

ROLE OF MINISTER CLEARLY DEFINED IN, each person who
has an office to perform, minister or layman, should do
all of, but only, those parts which pertain to his office
by the nature of the rite and the principles of the
liturgy: *in celebrationibus liturgicis quisque, sive min-*
ister sive fidelis, munere suo fungens, solum et totum
id agat, quod ad ipsum ex rei natura et normis liturgicis
pertinet (28).

SACRAMENTALS AS PART OF, whose purpose is to dispose
men to receive the chief effect of the sacraments: *Sacra-*
mentalia . . . per ea homines ad praecipuum Sacra-
mentorum effectum suscipiendum disponuntur (60).

SACRAMENTS AS PART OF, their purpose is to sanctify men,
to build up the body of Christ, and finally, to give
worship to God: *Sacramenta ordinantur ad sanctifica-*
tionem hominum, ad aedificationem Corporis Christi,
ad cultum denique Deo reddendum (59).

SACRED MUSIC AND, forms a necessary or integral part:
Musica . . . necessariam vel integralem liturgicae sol-
lemnis partem efficit (112).

SACRED SCRIPTURE AND, is of the greatest importance:
Maximum est sacrae Scripturae momentum in Liturgia
celebranda (24).

to achieve the restoration, progress, and adaptation of
the sacred liturgy, it is essential to promote a warm
and living love for it: *ad procurandam sacrae Litur-*
giae instaurationem, progressum et aptationem,
oportet ut promoveatur ille suavis et vivus sacrae
Scripturae affectus (24).

SANCTIFICATION EFFECTED IN, it moves the faithful, filled
with "the paschal sacraments," to be "one in holiness":
Vicissim, ipsa Liturgia impellit fideles ut "sacramentis
paschalibus" satiati fiant "pietate concordes" (10).

SERMON AND, to be highly esteemed as part of it: *Homilia*
. . . ut pars ipsius liturgiae valde commendatur (52).

SOLEMNLY CELEBRATED, in song, with the assistance of
sacred ministers and the active participation of the

people: *Formam nobiliorem actio liturgica accipit, cum divina Officia sollemniter in cantu celebrantur, quibus ministri sacri intersint quaeque populus actuose participet (113).*

SUBJECT TO HIERARCHY, it depends solely on the authority of the Church, that is, on the Apostolic See and, as laws may determine, on the bishop: *Sacrae Liturgiae moderatio ab Ecclesiae auctoritate unice pendet: quae quidem est apud Apostolicam Sedem et, ad normam iuris, apud Episcopum (22:1).*

in virtue of power conceded by the law, its regulation within certain defined limits belongs also to various kinds of competent territorial bodies of bishops legitimately established: *Ex potestate a iure concessa, rei liturgicae moderatio inter limites statutos pertinet quoque ad competentes varii generis territoriales Episcoporum coetus legitime constitutos (22:2).*

SUPERIOR TO OTHER ACTIONS, because it is an action of Christ the priest and of His body which is the Church. No other action of the Church can equal its efficacy by the same title and to the same degree: *Proinde omnis liturgica celebratio, utpote opus Christi sacerdotis, eiusque Corporis, quod est Ecclesia, est actio sacra praecellenter, cuius efficacitatem eodem titulo eodemque gradu nulla alia actio Ecclesiae adaequat (7).*

ULTIMATE DISTINCTIVE QUALITY OF, the primary and indispensable source from which the faithful are to derive the true Christian spirit: *est enim primus, isque necessarius fons, e quo spiritum vere christianum fideles hauriant (14).*

UNAUTHORIZED INNOVATIONS IN, forbidden to any person, even if he be a priest: *nemo omnino alius, etiamsi sit sacerdos quidquam proprio marte in Liturgia addat, demat, aut mutet (22:3).*

UNIFYING EFFECTS OF, it shows forth the Church to those who are outside as a sign lifted up among the nations under which the scattered children of God may be gathered together until there is one sheepfold and one shepherd: *Ecclesiam iis qui sunt foris ostendit ut signum levatum in nationes sub quo filii Dei dispersi congregentur in unum quousque unum ovile fiat et unus pastor (2).*

VALUE OF, is the most outstanding means whereby the faithful may express in their lives, and manifest to others, the mystery of Christ and the real nature of the true Church: *Liturgia . . . summe eo confert ut fideles vivendo exprimant et aliis manifestent mysterium Christi et genuinam verae Ecclesiae naturam (2).*

VERNACULAR AND, may frequently be of great advantage to the people, and the limits of its employment may be extended, whether in the Mass, the administration of the sacraments, or other parts: *Cum tamen, sive in Missa, sive in Sacramentorum administratione, sive in aliis Liturgiae partibus, haud raro linguae vernaculae usurpatio valde utilis apud populum exsistere possit, amplior locus ipsi tribui valeat (36:2).*

MANKIND, INTERCESSION ON BEHALF OF, is to be made in the restored "common prayer" in the Mass: *"Oratio communis" seu "fidelium" post Evangelium et homiliam, praesertim diebus dominicis et festis de praecepto, restituatur, ut, populo eam participante, obsecrationes fiant pro sancta Ecclesia, pro iis qui nos in potestate regunt, pro iis qui variis premuntur necessitatibus, ac pro omnibus hominibus totiusque mundi salute (53).*

MARRIAGE, FLEXIBILITY OF RITE OF, to be determined by the competent ecclesiastical authority mentioned in Art. 22:2 of this Constitution, which is free to draw up its own rite suited to the usages of place and people, according to the provision of Art. 63. But the rite must always conform to the law that the priest assisting at the marriage must ask for and obtain the consent of the contracting parties: *competenti auctoritati ecclesiasticae territoriali, de qua in art. 22:2 huius Constitutionis, relinquitur facultas, ad normam art. 63, exarandi ritum proprium usibus locorum et populorum congruentem, firma tamen lege ut sacerdos assistens requirat excipiatque contrahentium consensum (77).*

NUPTIAL BLESSING OUTSIDE OF MASS, always to be given: *Si Sacramentum Matrimonii sine Missa celebratur . . . benedictio sponsis semper impertiatur (78).*

OUTSIDE OF MASS, is to use the epistle and gospel from the nuptial Mass at the beginning of the ceremony: *Si Sacramentum Matrimonii sine Missa celebratur, Epistola et Evangelium Missae pro sponsis legantur in initio ritus (78).*

PRAYER FOR BRIDE IN CEREMONY OF, to be amended: *Oratio super sponsam, ita opportune emendata ut aequalia officia mutuae fidelitatis utriusque sponsi inculcet (78).*

REGIONAL CUSTOMS OF, to be retained: *Si quae provinciae aliis laudabilibus consuetudinibus et caeremoniis in celebrando Matrimonii Sacramento utuntur, eas omnino retineri Sancta Synodus vehementer optat (77).*

RITE OF, to be revised: *Ritus celebrandi Matrimonium, qui exstat in Rituali romano, recognoscatur et ditior fiat, quo clarius gratia Sacramenti significetur et munera coniugum inculcentur (77).*

TIME OF CEREMONY IN MASS, after the reading of the gospel and the homily, and before "the prayer of the faithful": *Matrimonium ex more intra Missam celebretur, post lectionem Evangelii et homiliam, ante "orationem fidelium" (78).*

VERNACULAR IN PRAYER FOR THE BRIDE, may be used: *Oratio super sponsam dici potest lingua vernacula (78).*

MARTYRS, ACCOUNTS OF, IN THE DIVINE OFFICE, are to accord with the facts of history: *Passiones seu vitae Sanctorum fidei historiae reddantur (92.c).*

FEASTS OF, occupy a place in the annual cycle. The
Church proposes them to the faithful as an example
to honor and imitate and also to seek their intercession:
*Memorias insuper Martyrum aliorumque Sanctorum,
qui per multiformem Dei gratiam ad perfectionem
provecti, atque aeternam iam adepti salutem, Deo in
caelis laudem perfectam decantant ac pro nobis inter-
cedunt circulo anni inseruit Ecclesia. In Sanctorum
enim nataliciis praedicat paschale mysterium in Sanctis
cum Christo compassis et conglorificatis, et fidelibus
exempla eorum proponit, omnes per Christum ad Patrem trahentia, eorumque meritis Dei beneficia impetrat*
(104).

MARY, BLESSED VIRGIN, LITURGICAL CULT OF, occupies a
preeminent place in the annual cycle of the Church's
feasts: *In hoc annuo mysteriorum Christi circulo celebrando, Sancta Ecclesia Beatam Mariam Dei Genetricem
cum peculiari amore veneratur, quae indissolubili nexu
cum Filii sui opere salutari coniungitur; in qua praecel-
lentem Redemptionis fructum miratur et exaltat, ac veluti
in purissima imagine, id quod ipsa tota esse cupit et sperat
cum gaudio contemplatur* (103).

MASS, AS A BANQUET, *Salvator noster, in Cena novissima,
qua nocte tradebatur, Sacrificium Eucharisticum Corporis
et Sanguinis sui instituit . . . convivium paschale, in
quo Christus sumitur, mens impletur gratia et futurae
gloriae nobis pignus datur* (47).

OF BAPTISM, COMMUNION UNDER BOTH SPECIES, may be
granted: *Communio sub utraque specie . . . neophytis in Missa quae Baptismum subsequitur* (55).

FOR BURIAL OF INFANTS, to be provided for: *propria Missa
pro sepeliendo parvulos donetur* (82).

CELEBRATION ALONE, is still the right of every priest:
*semper sit cuique sacerdoti facultas Missam singularem
celebrandi, non vero eodem tempore in eadem ecclesia,
nec feria V in Cena Domini* (57:2.2).

CEREMONIES OF, more than their observance is required of the pastor: *sacris pastoribus advigilandum est ut in actione liturgica non solum observentur leges ad validam et licitam celebrationem, sed ut fideles scienter, actuose et fructuose eandem participent (11).*

COMMEMORATION OF THE PASSION: *Salvator noster, in Cena novissima, qua nocte tradebatur, Sacrificium Eucharisticum Corporis et Sanguinis sui instituit, quo Sacrificium Crucis in saecula, donec veniret, perpetuaret, atque adeo Ecclessiae dilectae Sponsae memoriale concrederet Mortis et Resurrectionis suae (47).*

"THE COMMON PRAYER" IN THE VERNACULAR, is permitted: *Linguae vernaculae in Missis cum populo celebratis congruus locus tribui possit, praesertim in lectionibus et "oratione communi" (54).*

COMMUNAL FORMS OF RITES OF, involving the active participation of the faithful, are preferred to those that allow a celebration that is merely individual and quasi-private: *Quoties ritus, iuxta propriam cuiusque naturam, secum ferunt celebrationem communem, cum frequentia et actuosa participatione fidelium, inculcetur hanc, in quantum fieri potest, esse praeferendam celebrationi eorundem singulari et quasi privatae (27).*

COMMUNION CONSECRATED DURING THIS, is the more perfect form of participation: *Valde commendatur illa perfectior Missae participatio qua fideles post Communionem sacerdotis ex eodem Sacrificio Corpus Dominicum sumunt (55).*

CONCELEBRATION OF, is permitted in the following cases:

1. a) on the Thursday of the Lord's Supper, not only at the Mass of the Chrism, but also at the evening Mass;
   b) at Masses during councils, bishops' conferences, and synods;
   c) at the Mass for the blessing of an abbot.
2. Also, with permission of the ordinary, to whom it

belongs to decide whether concelebration is opportune:

a) at conventual Mass, and at the principal Mass in
   churches when the needs of the faithful do not
   require that all the priests available should celebrate individually;

b) at Masses celebrated at any kind of priests' meetings, whether the priests be secular clergy or
   religious.

Concelebratio permitti potest in sequentes casus:

1. a) *feria V in Cena Domini, tum ad Missam chris-
      matis, tum ad Missam vespertinam;*

   b) *ad Missas in Conciliis, Conventibus Episcopali-
      bus et Synodis;*

   c) *ad Missam in Benedictione Abbatis.*

2. *Praeterea, accedente licentia Ordinarii, cuius est de
   opportunitate concelebrationis iudicare:*

   a) *ad Missam conventualem et ad Missam princi-
      palem in ecclesiis, cum utilitas christifidelium
      singularem celebrationem omnium sacerdotum
      praesentium non postulat;*

   b) *ad Missas in conventibus cuiusvis generis sacer-
      dotum tum saecularium tum religiosorum (57:1).*

CONFIRMATION IN, may be allowed: *Confirmatio, pro opportunitate, intra Missam conferri potest (71).*

EXTENDED USE OF VERNACULAR IN, is allowed, but the
regulation laid down in Art. 40 of this Constitution is
to be observed: *amplior usus linguae vernaculae in
Missa opportunus esse videatur, servetur praescriptum
art. 40 huius constitutionis (54).*

FOR THE CONFERRING OF BAPTISM, to be inserted into the
Roman Missal: *Missali romano Missa propria "In collatione Baptismi" inseratur (66).*

IDEAL TO ACHIEVE IN REVISING RITE OF, a clearer manifestation of the intrinsic nature and purpose of its several parts, and also the connection between them, so

that the faithful may be able to more devoutly and actively participate: *Ordo Missae ita recognoscatur, ut singularum partium propria ratio necnon mutua connexio clarius pateant, atque pia et actuosa fidelium participatio facilior reddatur (50).*

LATIN IN, to be preserved in the Latin rites: *Linguae latinae usus, salvo particulari iure, in Ritibus latinis servetur (36:1).*

NATURE OF, is of itself public and social: *Missae celebratio . . . semper natura publica et sociali cuiusvis Missae (27).*

AS OFFERED BY THE FAITHFUL, the oblation which is primarily performed by the priest is also shared by them: *christifideles . . . immaculatam hostiam non tantum per sacerdotis manus, sed etiam una cum ipso offerentes, seipsos offere (48).*

ORDINARY OF, provisions to be made so that the parts which pertain to the people may also be recited or sung in Latin: *Provideatur tamen ut christifideles etiam lingua latina partes Ordinarii Missae quae ad ipsos spectant possint simul dicere vel cantare (54).*

OF ORDINATION, COMMUNION UNDER BOTH SPECIES, may be granted: *Communio sub utraque specie . . . ordinatis in Missa sacra suae ordinationis (55).*

PARTICIPATION IN, is the duty and right of the faithful by reason of their baptism: *participationem . . . vi Baptismatis ius habet et officium (14).*

by acclamations, responses, psalmody, antiphons, and songs, as well as by actions, gestures, and bodily attitudes: *Ad actuosam participationem promovendam, populi acclamationes, responsiones, psalmodia, antiphonae, cantica, necnon actiones seu gestus et corporis habitus foveantur (30). (cf. also 114.)*

by Communion consecrated during the same Mass: *Valde commendatur illa perfectior Missae participatio qua fideles post Communionem sacerdotis ex eodem Sacrificio Corpus Dominicum sumunt (55).*

by good understanding of the rites and prayers: *per ritus et preces id bene intellegentes, sacram actionem conscie, pie et actuose participent (48).*

by offering the immaculate victim, not only through the hands of the priest, but also with him: *immaculatam hostiam, non tantum per sacerdotis manus, sed etiam una cum ipso offerentes, seipsos offerre (48)*

by proper dispositions, so that the liturgy may be able to produce its full effects: *Ut haec tamen plena efficacitas habeatur, necessarium est ut fideles cum recti animi dispositionibus ad sacram Liturgiam accedant (11).*

is the earnest desire of Mother Church: *Valde cupit Mater Ecclesia ut fideles universi ad plenam illam, consciam atque actuosam liturgicarum celebrationum participationem ducantur, quae ab ipsius Liturgiae natura postulatur (14).*

PLURAL PRAYER FORMS IN, are addressed to God by the priest who presides over the assembly in the person of Christ in the name of the entire holy people and of all present: *preces a sacerdote, qui coetui in persona Christi praeest, ad Deum directae, nomine totius plebis sanctae et omnium circumstantium dicuntur (33).*

PRESENCE OF CHRIST IN, not only in the person of His minister, "the same now offering, through the ministry of priests, who formerly offered Himself on the cross," but especially under the eucharistic species: *praesens adest in Missae Sacrificio cum in ministri persona* "idem nunc offerens sacerdotum ministerio, qui seipsum tunc in cruce obtulit," *tum maxime sub speciebus eucharisticis (7).*

RELIGIOUS PROFESSION WITHIN, new rite to be drawn up, apart from exceptions in particular law, and adopted: *Conficiatur praeterea ritus professionis religiosae et renovationis votorum . . . ab iis qui professionem vel*

votorum renovationem *intra Missam peragunt, salvo
iure particulari assumendus (80).*

RITE OF, to be revised in such a way that the intrinsic
nature and purpose of its several parts, as also the connection between them, may be more clearly manifested,
and that devout and active participation by the faithful
may be more easily achieved: *Ordo Missae ita recognoscatur, ut singularum partium propria ratio necnon
mutua connexio clarius pateant, atque pia et actuosa
fidelium participatio facilior reddatur (50).*

RITES, that make provision, according to their specific
nature, for communal celebration involving the presence and active participation of the faithful, are to be
preferred: *quoties ritus, iuxta propriam cuiusque naturam, secum ferunt celebrationem communem, cum
frequentia et actuosa participatione fidelium, inculcetur hanc, in quantum fieri potest, esse praeferendam (27).*

SERMON, to be highly esteemed as part of the liturgy:
*Homilia . . . ut pars ipsius liturgiae valde commen-
datur (52).*

SUNDAY AND HOLY DAYS, COMMON PRAYER, to be restored,
after the gospel and the homily: *"Oratio communis,"
seu "fidelium," post Evangelium et homiliam, praesertim diebus dominicis et festis de praecepto, restituatur (53).*

> PARTICIPATION, especially on these days is to be strongly
> encouraged by pastors: *Sacra proinde Synodus ve-
> hementer hortatur animarum pastores ut, in cate-
> chesi tradenda, fideles sedulo doceant de integra
> Missa participanda praesertim diebus dominicis et
> festis de praecepto (56).*

> SERMON, not to be omitted on these days except for a
> serious reason: *Homilia . . . quinimmo in Missis
> quae diebus dominicis et festis de praecepto con-
> currente populo celebrantur, ne omittatur, nisi gravi
> de causa (52).*

Communion under both species may be granted: *Communio sub utraque specie . . . professis in Missa religiosae suae professionis (55)*.

TIME OF MATRIMONY IN, after the reading of the gospel and the homily, and before "the prayer of the faithful": *Matrimonium ex more intra Missam celebretur, post lectionem Evangelii et homiliam, ante "orationem fidelium" (78)*.

VERNACULAR IN, to apply in the first place to the readings and "the common prayer" or "the prayer of the faithful," and also, as local conditions may warrant, to those parts which pertain to the people, according to the norm laid down in Art. 36 of this Constitution: *Linguae vernaculae in Missis cum populo celebratis congruus locus tribui possit, praesertim in lectionibus et "oratio communi," ac, pro condicione locorum, etiam in partibus quae ad populum spectant, ad normam art. 36 huius Constitutionis (54)*.

MATINS, to be adapted so that it may be recited at any hour of the day: *hora quae Matutinum vocatur . . . ita accommodetur ut qualibet diei hora recitari possit (89.c)*.
to be made up of fewer psalms and longer readings: *Hora quae Matutinum vocatur . . . psalmis paucioribus lectionibusque longioribus constet (89.c)*.

MERCY, WORKS OF, BY MEANS OF, the formation of the faithful is completed in the various seasons of the year: *Variis denique anni temporibus . . . Ecclesia fidelium eruditionem perficit . . . per misericordiae opera (105)*.

MINISTERS IN LITURGICAL CELEBRATIONS, exercise a genuine liturgical function: *Etiam ministrantes . . . vero ministerio liturgico funguntur (29)*.

MISSAL, ROMAN, NEW RITE FOR CONCELEBRATION, to be drawn up and inserted: *Novus ritus concelebrationis conficiatur . . . Missali Romano inserendus (58)*.
SPECIAL MASS "FOR CONFERRING OF BAPTISM" to be in-

serted: *Missali romano Missa propria "In collatione Baptismi" inseratur (66)*.

MISSION LANDS, INITIATION RITES OF, when capable of being adapted to Christian ritual may be admitted along with those already found in Christian tradition: *In terris Missionum, praeter ea quae in traditione christiana habentur, illa etiam elementa initiationis admitti liceat, quae apud unumquemque populum in usu esse reperiuntur quatenus ritui christiano accommodari possunt (65)*.

LITURGICAL BOOKS AND, when revised, are to provide for legitimate variations and adaptations to different groups, regions, and peoples, provided that the substantial unity of the Roman rite is preserved: *Servata substantiali unitate ritus romani, legitimis varietatibus et aptationibus ad diversos coetus, regiones, populos, praesertim in Missionibus, locus relinquatur, etiam cum libri recognoscuntur (38)*.

NATIVE MUSIC OF, a suitable place is to be given to it, not only in forming the attitude of the people toward religion, but also in adapting worship to their native genius: *Cum in regionibus quibusdam, praesertim Missionum, gentes inveniantur quibus propria est traditio musica . . . huic musicae aestimatio debita necnon locus congruus praebeatur, tam in fingendo earum sensu religioso, quam in cultu ad earum indolem accommodando (119)*.

SHORTER RITE OF INFANT BAPTISM, to be drawn up to be used by catechists: *Conficiatur item Ordo brevior (Baptismi) quo, praesertim in terris Missionum, catechistae . . . uti possint (68)*.

MISSIONARIES, MUSICAL TRAINING OF, to qualify them to become competent in promoting the traditional music of the native peoples, both in schools and in sacred services, as far as possible: *Quapropter in institutione musica* missionariorum diligenter curetur, ut, quantum fieri potest, traditionalem earum gentium musicam tam in scholis quam in actionibus sacris promovere valeant *(119)*.

MONKS, ORDERS OF, DIVINE OFFICE AND, are obliged to celebrate the entire office in choir every day in addition to the conventual Mass: *Communitates choro obligatae, praeter Missam conventualem, tenentur Officium divinum cotidie in choro celebrare, et quidem . . . totum officium . . . Ordines Monachorum (95.a)*.

MOTHER TONGUE. See VERNACULAR.

MUSIC, CHANT BOOKS, a more critical edition is to be prepared of those already published since the restoration of Pius X: *paretur editio magis critica librorum iam editorum post instaurationem sancti Pii X (117)*.

an edition containing simpler melodies for use in small churches should be prepared: *Expedit quoque ut paretur editio simpliciores modos continens, in usum minorum ecclesiarum (117)*.

CHOIRS, to be diligently promoted, especially in cathedral churches: *Scholae cantorum assidue provehantur, praesertim apud ecclesias cathedrales (114)*.

members exercise a genuine liturgical function: *Ii qui ad scholam cantorum pertinent, vero ministerio liturgico funguntur (29)*.

CHURCH'S TREASURY OF, to be preserved and fostered with great care: *Thesaurus Musicae sacrae summa cura servetur et foveatur (114)*.

COMMISSION OF, to be established in every diocese, as far as possible: *in quavis dioecesi constituantur, quantum fieri potest, etiam Commissiones de Musica sacra (46)*.

COMPOSERS OF, to cultivate and increase its store of treasures: *Sentiant musicae artifices, spiritu christiano imbuti, se ad Musicam sacram colendam et ad thesaurum eius augendum esse vocatos (121)*.

to produce compositions which have the qualities proper to genuine sacred music: *Modos autem com-*

> > *ponant, qui notas verae Musicae sacrae prae se
> > ferant (121).*

to produce compositions not only for large choirs, but also for small choirs and for the active participation of the entire assembly of the faithful: *non solum a maioribus scholis cantorum cani possint, sed minoribus quoque scholis conveniant et actuosam participationem totius coetus fidelium foveant (121).*

to be trained in liturgy: *Musicae vero artifices . . . etiam germana institutione liturgica donentur (115).*

CONGREGATIONAL SINGING, to be skilfully fostered: *cantus popularis religiosus sollertur foveatur (118). (cf. also 114.)*

EXPERTS IN, to assist the liturgical commission set up by the competent territorial ecclesiastical authority mentioned in Art. 22:2: *A competenti auctoritate ecclesiastica territoriali, de qua in art. 22:2, expedit ut instituatur Commissio liturgica, a viris in . . . Musica . . . peritis iuvanda (44).*

EXTOLLED BY THE CHURCH, holy scripture indeed has bestowed praise upon it, and the same may be said of the fathers of the Church and of the Roman pontiffs: *profecto sacros concentus laudibus extulerunt cum Sacra Scriptura, tum sancti Patres atque Romani Pontifices (112).*

GREGORIAN CHANT, is Church's own, being acknowledged as specially suited to the Roman liturgy, and therefore, other things being equal, should be given preference in liturgical services: *Ecclesia cantum gregorianum agnoscit ut liturgiae romanae proprium: qui ideo in actionibus liturgicis, ceteris paribus, principem locum obtineat (116).*

INFLUENCE ON THE LITURGY, embellishes it in a more noble way when the divine offices are celebrated solemnly in song, with the assistance of sacred ministers and the active participation of the people: *Formam nobiliorem actio liturgica accipit, cum divina Officia sollemniter in cantu celebrantur, quibus ministri sacri intersint quaeque populus actuose participet (113).*

INSTITUTE OF, to be established whenever this can be done: *Commendantur insuper Instituta Superiora de Musica sacra pro opportunitate erigenda (115).*

INSTRUMENTS OF, may be admitted for use in divine worship, with the knowledge and consent of the competent territorial authority, as laid down in Art. 22:2, 37 and 40: *Alia vero instrumenta, de iudicio et consensu auctoritatis territorialis competentis, ad normam art. 22:2, 37 et 40, in cultum divinum admittere licet (120).*

    to be admitted into divine worship they must be suitable, or can be made suitable, for sacred use, accord with the dignity of the temple, and truly contribute to the edification of the faithful: *instrumenta . . . in cultum divinum admittere licet, quatenus usui sacro apta sint aut aptari possint, templi dignitati congruant, atque revera aedificationi fidelium faveant (120).*

LANGUAGE AND, in this regard provisions of Art. 26 are to observed; for the Mass, Art. 54; for the sacraments, Art. 63; for the Divine Office, Art. 101: *Quoad linguam adhibendam, serventur praecepta art. 36; quoad Missam art. 54; quoad Sacramenta, art. 63; quoad Officium divinum, art. 101 (113).*

MINISTERIAL FUNCTION OF, it adds delight to prayer, fosters unity of minds, confers greater solemnity upon the sacred rites: *Musica sacra . . . sive orationem suavius exprimens vel unanimitatem fovens, sive ritus sacros maiore locupletans sollemnitate (112).*

MISSION LANDS AND, have their own traditions, and these play a great part in their religious and social life. For this reason due importance is to be attached to their music, and a suitable place is to be given to it, not only in forming the attitude of the peoples toward religion, but also in adapting worship to their native genius, as indicated in Art. 39 and 40: *Cum in regionibus quibus-*

dam, praesertim Missionum gentes inveniantur quibus
propria est traditio musica, magnum momentum in
earum vita religiosa ac sociali habens, huic musicae
aestimatio debita necnon locus congruus praebeatur,
tam in fingendo earum sensu religioso, quam in cultu
ad earum indolem accommodando, ad mentem art.
39 et 40 (119).

NATURE OF, it forms a necessary or integral part of the
solemn liturgy: Musica . . . eo praesertim quod ut
cantus sacer qui verbis inhaeret necessariam vel integralem liturgiae sollemnis partem efficit (112).

NORM FOR, it is considered more holy in proportion as it
is more closely connected with the liturgical action:
Ideo Musica sacra tanto sanctior erit quanto arctius
cum actione liturgica connectetur (112).

PASTORAL CARE FOR, bishops and other pastors of souls
must be at pains to ensure that, whenever the sacred
action is to be celebrated with song, the whole body of
the faithful may be able to contribute that active participation which is rightly theirs, as laid down in Art.
28 and 30: Episcopi vero ceterique animarum pastores
sedulo curent ut in qualibet actione sacra in cantu peragenda universus fidelium coetus actuosam participationem sibi propriam praestare valeat, ad normam art.
28 et 30 (114).

POLYPHONIC FORMS, are admitted in the liturgical celebrations so long as they accord with the spirit of the liturgical action, as laid down in Art. 30: Alia genera
Musicae sacrae, praesertim vero polyphonia, in celebrandi divinis Officiis minime excluduntur, dummodo
spiritui actionis liturgicae respondeant, ad normam art.
30 (116).

IN SEMINARIES, great importance is to be attached to its
teaching, as well as in other Catholic institutions and
schools: Magni habeatur institutio et praxis musica
in Seminariis, in Religiosorum utriusque sexus noviti-

*atibus et studiorum domibus, necnon in ceteris insti-
tutis et scholis catholicis (115).*

TEXTS OF, to conform with Catholic doctrine: *Textus
cantui sacro destinati catholicae doctrinae sint conformes (121).*

to be drawn chiefly from holy scripture and from liturgical sources: *ex Sacris Scripturis et fontibus liturgicis potissimum hauriantur (121).*

TRADITIONAL INSTRUMENT OF, in the Latin Church is
the pipe organ: *Organum tubulatum in Ecclesia latina
magno in honore habeatur, tamquam instrumentum
musicum traditionale (120).*

TRAINING OF MISSIONARIES IN, every effort should be made
so that they become competent in promoting the traditional music of mission peoples both in schools and
in sacred services, as far as may be possible: *Quapropter
in institutione musica missionariorum, diligenter curetur ut, quantum fieri potest, traditionalem earum gentium musicam tam in scholis quam in actionibus sacris
promovere valeant (119).*

TRAINING OF SEMINARY PROFESSORS, and professors of
other Catholic institutions, is to be carefully undertaken: *musica in Seminariis . . . ad quam quidem institutionem assequendam, magistri, qui Musicae sacrae
docendae praeficiuntur, sedulo conformentur (115).*

TYPICAL EDITION OF CHANT BOOKS, to be completed:
*Compleatur editio typica librorum cantus gregoriani
(117).*

MYSTERIES OF THE FAITH, to be expounded in the
homily during the course of the liturgical year: *Homilia,
qua per anni liturgici cursum ex textu sacro fidei mysteria
. . . exponuntur (52).*

MYSTERY OF CHRIST, is unfolded by the Church within the cycle of a year: *Totum vero Christi mysterium per
anni circulum explicat (102).*

OF FAITH, intelligent participation when present, is the earnest desire of the Church: *itaque Ecclesia sollicitas curas eo intendit ne christifideles huic fidei mysterio tamquam extranei vel muti spectatores intersint, sed . . . bene intellegentes . . . pie et actuose participent (48).*

MYSTICAL BODY, CHRIST AS HEAD OF, associates the Church with Himself in glorifying God and sanctifying men. The Church is His beloved Bride who calls to her Lord, and through Him offers worship to the Eternal Father: *Reapse tanto in opere quo Deus perfecte glorificatur, et homines sanctificantur, Christus Ecclesiam, sponsam suam dilectissimam, sibi semper consciat, quae Dominum suum invocat et per ipsum Aeterno Patri cultum tribuit (7).*

DIVINE OFFICE, all who render this service are not only fulfilling a duty of the Church, but also are sharing in the greatest honor of Christ's spouse, for by offering these praises to God they are standing before God's throne in the name of the Church their Mother: *Omnes proinde qui haec praestant, tum Ecclesiae officium explent, tum summum Sponsae Christi honorem participant, quia laudes Deo persolventes stant antre thronum Dei nomine Mater Ecclesiae (85).*

LITURGY AS WORSHIP OF, which is performed by the Head and His members: *Liturgia . . . a mystico Iesu Christi Corpore, Capite nempe eiusque membris, integer cultus publicus exercetur (7).*

AS SYNONYMOUS WITH THE CHURCH, Christ continues His priestly work through the agency of His Church, which is ceaselessly engaged in praising the Lord and interceding for the salvation of the whole world: *Christus Iesus . . . illud enim sacerdotale munus per ipsam Ecclesiam pergit . . . Dominum sine intermissione laudat et pro totius mundi salute interpellat (83).*

Nᴀᴛɪᴠᴇ ᴄᴜsᴛᴏᴍs, ʙᴜʀɪᴀʟ ᴏꜰ ᴅᴇᴀᴅ ᴀɴᴅ, to correspond more closely to the circumstances and traditions
found in the various regions. This holds good for the liturgical color to be used: *ritus exsequiarum . . . condicionibus et traditionibus singularum regionum etiam
quoad colorem liturgicam, melius respondeat (81).*

ɪɴɪᴛɪᴀᴛɪᴏɴ ʀɪᴛᴇs ᴀɴᴅ, elements from these, when capable
of being adapted to Christian ritual, may be admitted
along with those already found in Christian tradition:
*in terris Missionum . . . praeter ea quae in traditione
christiana habentur, illa etiam elementa initiationis admitti liceat . . . quatenus ritui christiano accommodari possunt, ad normam art. 37–40 huius Constitutionis (65).*

ʟɪᴛᴜʀɢɪᴄᴀʟ ʙᴏᴏᴋs ᴀɴᴅ, provisions to be made for legitimate variations and adaptations to different groups,
regions, and peoples, especially in mission lands, provided that the substantial unity of the Roman rite is
preserved: *Servata substantiali unitate ritus romani,
legitimis varietatibus et aptationibus ad diversos coetus,
regiones, populos, praesertim in Missionibus, locus relinquatur, etiam cum libri liturgici recognoscuntur (38).*

ʟɪᴛᴜʀɢʏ ᴀɴᴅ, to be admitted as long as they are not indissolubly bound up with superstition and error:
*quidquid vero in populorum moribus indissolubili vin-
culo superstitionibus erroribusque non adstipulatur
. . . immo quandoque in ipsam Liturgiam admittit
(37).*

Nᴀᴛɪᴠᴇ ᴍᴜsɪᴄ, ʟɪᴛᴜʀɢʏ ᴀɴᴅ, in certain parts of the
world, especially mission lands, there are peoples who
have their own musical traditions. . . . A suitable place
is to be given to it in adapting worship to their native
genius, as indicated in Art. 39 and 40: *Cum in regionibus
quibusdam, praesertim Missionum, gentes inveniantur
quibus propria est traditio musica . . . huic . . . locus*

congruus praebeatur . . . quam in cultu ad earum indolem accommodando ad mentem art. 39 et 40 (119).

NEWLY BAPTIZED, COMMUNION UNDER BOTH SPECIES,
may be granted, when the bishop thinks fit: *Communio
sub utraque specie . . . concedi potest, de iudicio Episcoporum . . . neophytis in Missa quae Baptismum subsequitur (55).*

NEWLY ORDAINED, COMMUNION UNDER BOTH SPECIES,
may be granted, when the bishop thinks fit: *Communio
sub utraque specie . . . concedi potest, de iudicio Episcoporum, veluti ordinatis in Missa sacra suae ordinationis
(55).*

NEWLY PROFESSED, COMMUNION UNDER BOTH SPE-
CIES, may be granted, when the bishop thinks fit: *Communio sub utraque specie . . . concedi potest, de iudicio
Episcoporum . . . professis in Missa religiosae suae professionis (55).*

NON-CLERICAL INSTITUTES, DIVINE OFFICE AND,
they perform the public prayer of the Church, those who
recite any parts of the Divine Office according to their
constitution: *Sodales cuiusvis Instituti status perfectionis, qui, vi Constitutionum, partes aliquas divini Officii
absolvunt, orationem publicam Ecclesiae agunt (98).*

the competent superior has the power to grant the use
of the vernacular, even in choir: *sodalibus, sive viris
non clericis sive mulieribus . . . in Officio divino,
etiam in choro celebrando, concedi potest a Superiore competente ut lingua vernacula utantur,
dummodo versio approbata sit (101:2).*

NONE, IN CHOIR, to be observed: *In choro Horae minores
. . . Nona serventur (89.e).*

OUTSIDE OF CHOIR, it is lawful to select any one of the
three hours, according to the respective hour of the
day: *Extra chorum e tribus unam seligere licet, diei
tempori magis congruentem (89.e).*

NUNS, ORDERS OF, DIVINE OFFICE AND, who are bound by law or constitution to choral office must celebrate the entire office: *totum Officium Ordines . . . Monialium . . . ex iure vel constitutionibus choro adstrictorum* (95.a).

> are bound to recite individually those canonical hours which they do not pray in choir: *omnes autem illarum Communitatum sodales, qui sunt solemniter professi . . . debent eas Horas canonicas soli recitare, quas in choro non persolvunt (95.c).*

NUPTIAL BLESSING, IN THE VERNACULAR, is permitted: *oratio super sponsam . . . dici potest lingua vernacula (78).*

> OUTSIDE OF MASS, should always be given: *Si vero Sacramentum Matrimonii sine Missa celebratur . . . benedictio sponsis semper impertiatur (78).*

NUPTIAL MASS, FORM OF PRAYER FOR BRIDE, to be amended: *Oratio super sponsam, ita opportune emendata (78).*

> TIME OF MATRIMONY, after the reading of the gospel and the homily, and before "the prayer of the faithful": *Matrimonium ex more intra Missam celebretur, post lectionem Evangelii et homiliam, ante "orationem fidelium" (78).*

OFFERING, PARTICIPATION OF LAITY IN, not only through the hands of the priest, but also with him, they should learn also to offer themselves: *huic fidei mysterio . . . non tantum per sacerdotis manus, sed etiam una cum ipso offerentes, seipsos offerre discant (48).*

OFFICE, DIVINE. See DIVINE OFFICE.

ORATIO FIDELIUM. See COMMON PRAYER.

"ORDER OF SUPPLYING WHAT WAS OMITTED IN INFANT BAPTISM," RITE OF, to be revised: *loco*

ritus qui "Ordo supplendi omissa super infantem baptizatum" appellatur, novus conficiatur (69).

ORDINARIES, FACULTIES AND DUTIES OF, to dispense their
subjects, in particular cases, and for a just reason, from
the obligation of reciting the Divine Office, wholly or in
part, or to commute it: *In casibus singularibus iustaque
de causa, Ordinarii possunt subditos suos ab obligatione
Officium recitandi ex toto vel ex parte dispensare vel id
commutare (97).*

to exercise good taste in sacred art, striving after noble
beauty rather than mere sumptuous display. This
principle applies also in the matter of sacred vestments and ornaments: *Curent Ordinarii ut artem
vere sanctam promoventes eique faventes, potius
nobilem intendat pulchritudinem quam meram
sumptuositatem. Quod etiam intellegatur de sacris
vestibus et ornamentis (124).*

to grant the use of a vernacular translation of the
Divine Office, in individual cases, to those clerics
for whom the use of the Latin constitutes a grave
obstacle to their praying the office properly: *facta
tamen Ordinarii potestate usum versionis vernaculae
ad normam art. 36 confectae concedendi, singulis
pro casibus, iis clericis, quibus usus linguae latinae
grave impedimentum est quominus Officium debite
persolvant (101:1).*

to permit concelebration in the following cases:

a) at Conventual Mass, and at the principal Mass in
churches when the needs of the faithful do not
require that all the priests available should celebrate individually;

b) at Masses celebrated at any kind of priests' meetings, whether the priests be secular clergy or religious.

*Accedente licentia Ordinarii, cuius est de opportuni-
tate concelebrationis iudicare:*

    a) *ad Missam conventualem et ad Missam princi-*
    palem in ecclesiis, cum utilitas christifidelium sin-
    gularem celebrationem omnium sacerdotum
    praesentium non postulat;

    b) *ad Missas in conventibus cuiusvis generis sacer-*
    dotum tum saecularium tum religiosorum (57:1.
    2.a.b).

ORDINARIES, LOCAL, DUTIES OF, TO HAVE SPECIAL CON-
CERN FOR SACRED FURNISHINGS AND WORKS OF VALUE, lest
they be disposed of or dispersed: *sedulo advigilent Ordi-*
narii ne sacra supellex vel opera pretiosa, utpote orna-
menta domus Dei, alienentur vel disperdantur (126).

    TO JUDGE WORKS OF ART, and in so doing to give a hear-
    ing to the diocesan commission on sacred art, and if
    needed, also to others who are especially expert, and to
    the commissions referred to in Art. 44, 45 and 46: *In*
    diiudicandis artis operibus Ordinarii locorum audiant
    Commissionem dioecesanam de Arte sacra, et, si casus
    ferat, alios viros valde peritos, necnon Commissiones
    de quibus in articulis 44, 45, 46 (126).

    TO REGULATE THE RESTORED CATECHUMENATE for adults:
    Instauretur catechumenatus adultorum . . . de iu-
    dicio Ordinarii loci in usum deducendus (64).

    TO REGULATE THE USE OF VARIANTS CONTAINED IN THE
    BAPTISMAL RITE: *In ritu Baptismi ne desint accommo-*
    dationes, de iudicio Ordinarii loci adhibendae (68).

ORDINARY OF THE MASS, steps should be taken so
that the faithful may be able to say or sing together in
Latin those parts which pertain to them: *Provideatur*
tamen ut christifideles etiam lingua latina partes Ordi-
narii Missae quae ad ipsos spectant possint simul dicere
vel cantare (54).

ORDINATION, BISHOP'S ALLOCUTION, may be in the vernacular: *Allocutio Episcopi, initio Ordinationis . . .*
fieri potest lingua vernacula (76).

CEREMONIES AND TEXTS, to be revised: *ritus Ordinationum, sive quoad caeremonias sive quoad textus, recognoscantur (76).*

COMMUNION UNDER BOTH SPECIES, may be permitted: *Communio sub utraque specie . . . concedi potest . . . veluti ordinatis in Missa sacrae suae ordinationis (55).*

ORGAN, PIPE, is the Latin Church's classical musical instrument: *Organum tubulatum in Ecclesia latina magno in honore habeatur (120).*

PAINTINGS, CHURCH'S RIGHT TO JUDGE, deciding which of the works of artists are in accordance with faith, piety, and cherished traditional laws, and thereby fitted for sacred use: *Immo earum veluti arbitram Ecclesia iure semper se habuit, diiudicans inter artificum opera quae fidei, pietati legibusque religiose traditis congruerent, atque ad usum sacrum idonea haberentur (122).*

FREEDOM OF EXPRESSION IN, admitted. The Church has not adopted any particular style of her own; she has admitted styles from every period according to the natural talents and circumstances of the peoples, and the needs of the various rites: *Ecclesia nullum artis stilum veluti proprium habuit, sed secundum gentium indoles ac condiciones atque variorum Rituum necessitates modos cuiusvis aetatis admisit (123).*

HIERARCHY AND, to exercise good taste: *Curent Ordinarii ut artem vere sacram promoventes eique faventes, potius nobilem intendant pulchritudinem quam meram sumptuositatem (124).*

to watch over, and carefully remove from the house of God and other sacred places those works of artists which are repugnant to faith, morals and Christian piety: *Curent Episcopi ut artificum opera, quae fidei et moribus, ac christianae pietati repugnent . . .*

ab aedibus Dei aliisque locis sacris sedulo arceantur
(124).

INFLUENCE IN WORSHIP, by their very nature they are
oriented toward the infinite beauty of God which they
attempt in some way to portray by the work of human
hands: *ars religiosa . . . natura sua ad infinitam pul-*
chritudinem divinam spectant, humanis operibus ali-
quomodo exprimendam (122).

MODERN, allowed, provided that they adorn the sacred
buildings and holy rites with due reverence and honor:
Nostrorum etiam temporum atque omnium gentium et
regionum ars liberum in Ecclesia exercitium habeat,
dummodo sacris aedibus sacrisque ritibus debita rever-
entia debitoque honore inserviat (123).

PARENTS, ROLE OF, and also their duties, should be
brought out more clearly in the revised rite for the baptism of infants: *Ritus baptizandi parvulos recognoscatur*
. . . partes etiam parentum . . . eorumque officia, in
ipso ritu, magis pateant (67).

PARISH, THE, in some manner represents the visible
Church constituted throughout the world: *paroechiae*
sub pastore vices gerente Episcopi ordinatae, eminent:
nam quodammodo repraesentant Ecclesiam visibilem per
orbem terrarum constitutam (42).

COMMON PRAYER IN SUNDAY MASS, to be restored: "*Oratio*
communis" seu "*fidelium*" *post Evangelium et homi-*
liam, praesertim diebus dominicis et festis de prae-
cepto (53).

LITURGICAL LIFE OF, and its relationship to the bishop
must be fostered theoretically and practically among
the faithful and clergy: *vita liturgica paroeciae eiusque*
relatio ad Episcopum in mente et praxi fidelium et
cleri fovenda est (42).

SUNDAY MASS, should be a common celebration: *et adla-*
borandum ut sensus communitatis paroecialis, imprimis

vero *in communi celebratione Missae dominicalis, floreat (42)*.

SUNDAY SERMON, should not be omitted except for a serious reason: *Homilia . . . quinimmo in Missis quae diebus dominicis . . . concurrente populo celebrantur, ne omittatur, nisi gravi de causa (52)*.

SUNDAY VESPERS, should be celebrated in common: *Curent animarum pastores ut Horae praecipuae, praesertim Vesperae, diebus dominicis . . . in ecclesia communiter celebrentur (100)*.

PARTICIPATION, ACTIVE AND FULL, by all the people is the aim to be considered before all else in the restoration of the sacred liturgy: *Quae totius populi plena et actuosa participatio, in instauranda et fovenda sacra Liturgia, summopere est attendenda (14)*.

BAPTIZED AND, is their right and duty: *participationem . . . vi Baptismatis ius habet et officium (14)*.

DESIRE OF THE CHURCH, that all the faithful should be led to that full, conscious, and active participation which is demanded by the very nature of the liturgy: *Valde cupit Mater Ecclesia ut fideles universi ad plenam illam, consciam atque actuosam liturgicarum celebrationum participationem ducantur, quae ab ipsius Liturgiae natura postulatur (14)*.

PASTORS TO ENCOURAGE, it is their duty to ensure that the faithful take part fully aware of what they are doing, actively engaged in the rite, and enriched by its effects: *Ideo sacris pastoribus advigilandum est ut in actione liturgica . . . ut fideles scienter, actuose et fructose eandem participent (11)*.

they are to promote it both internally and externally, taking into account the age and condition of the faithful, their way of life, and standard of religious culture: *actuosam fidelium participationem, internam et externam, iuxta ipsorum aetatem, condicionem, vitae genus et religiosae culturae gradum,*

animarum pastores sedulo ac patienter prosequantur
(19).

they must zealously strive to achieve it by means of the
necessary instruction, in all their pastoral work: *et
ideo in tota actione pastorali, per debitam institutionem, ab animarum pastoribus est sedulo adpetenda (14).*

when instructing the faithful, they must insistently
teach them to take their part in the entire Mass,
especially on Sundays and feasts of obligation: *Sacra
proinde Synodus vehementer hortatur animarum
pastores ut, in catechesi tradenda, fideles sedulo doceant de integra Missa participanda, praesertim diebus dominicis et festis de praecepto (56).*

VARIOUS WAYS TO ACHIEVE, by means of acclamations, responses, psalmody, antiphons and songs, as well as by
actions, gestures, and bodily attitudes: *ad actuosam
participationem promovendam, populi acclamationes,
responsiones, psalmodia, antiphonae, cantica, necnon
actiones seu gestus et corporis habitus foveantur (30).*

by congregational singing: *cantus popularis religiosus
sollerter foveantur (118).*

by intelligent understanding of the rites and prayers:
*Ecclesia . . . intendit . . .   christifideles   huic
fidei mysterio . . . per ritus et preces id bene intellegentes, sacram actionem conscie, pie et actuose
participent (48).*

by listening to God's word: *verbo Deo instituantur
(48).*

by offering the immaculate victim through and with
the priest: *immaculatam hostiam, non tantum per
sacerdotis manus, sed etiam una cum ipso offerentes,
seipsos offerre discant (48).*

by proper dispositions: *Ut haec tamen plena efficacitas
habeatur, necessarium est ut fideles cum recti animi
dispositionibus ad sacram Liturgiam accedant (11).*

by receiving Communion consecrated during the same

sacrifice: *Valde commendatur illa perfectior Missae
participatio qua fideles post Communionem sacerdotis ex eodem Sacrificio Corpus Dominicum sumunt (55).*

PASCHAL MYSTERY, CHURCH AND, has never failed to
come together to celebrate: reading those things "which
were in all the scriptures concerning Him" (Luke 24:27),
celebrating the eucharist in which "the victory and tri-
umph of His death are again made present," and at the
same time giving thanks "to God for His unspeakable
gift" (2 Cor. 9:15) in Christ Jesus, "in praise of His
glory" (Eph. 1:12), through the power of the Holy Spirit:
*Numquam exinde omisit Ecclesia quin in unum conveni-
ret ad paschale mysterium celebrandum: legendo ea "in
omnibus Scripturis quae de ipso erant" (Lc. 24:27),
Eucharistiam celebrando in qua "mortis eius victoria et
triumphus repraesentatur," et simul gratias agendo "Deo
super inenarrabili dono" (2 Cor. 9:15) in Christo Iesu,
in laudem gloriae eius" (Eph. 1:12) per virtutem Spiritus
Sancti (6).*

SUNDAY CELEBRATION OF, is the tradition handed down
from the apostles which took its origin from the very
day of Christ's resurrection: *Mysterium paschale Ecclesia, ex traditione apostolica quae originem ducit ab
ipsa die Resurrectionis Christi, octava quaque die celebrat, quae dies Domini, seu dies dominica merito nun-
cupatur (106).*

PASTORAL-LITURGICAL ACTION, REGULATION OF,
by the territorial Liturgical Commission under the direction of the competent territorial ecclesiastical authority
mentioned in Art. 22:2: *A competenti auctoritate ecclesiastica territoriali, de qua in art. 22:2, expedit ut instituatur Commissio liturgica . . . Ipsius Commissionis
erit, ductu auctoritatis ecclesiasticae territorialis, de qua
supra, et actionem pastoralem liturgicam in sua dicione
moderari (44).*

PASTORAL LITURGY, INSTITUTE OF, to assist the territorial Commission for the Liturgy: *Cui Commissioni, in quantum fieri potest, opem ferat quoddam Institutum Liturgiae Pastoralis (44).*

PASTORAL THEOLOGY IN SEMINARIES, to be integrated with aspects of the liturgy: *Curent insuper aliarum disciplinarum magistri, imprimis . . . theologiae pastoralis . . . ut exinde earum connexio cum Liturgia . . . aperte clarescant (16).*

PASTORS, DUTIES OF, TO GIVE LITURGICAL INSTRUCTION, taking into account the age and condition of the people, their way of life, and standard of religious culture: *Liturgicam institutionem . . . iuxta ipsorum aetatem condicionem, vitae genus et religiosae culturae gradum, animarum pastores sedulo et patienter prosequantur (19).*

   TO BE IMBUED WITH THE SPIRIT AND POWER OF THE LITURGY, first themselves, if they hope to realize this in others: *Ut hoc evenire possit, nulla spes effulget nisi prius ipsi animarum pastores spiritu et virtute Liturgiae penitus imbuantur (14).*

   TO PROMOTE INTELLIGENT PARTICIPATION, so that the faithful will be fully aware of what they are doing, actively engaged in the rite, and enriched by its effects: *Ideo sacris pastoribus advigilandum est ut in actione liturgica non solum observentur leges ad validam et licitam celebrationem, sed ut fideles scienter, actuose et fructuose eandem participent (11).*

   TO PROVIDE FOR CONGREGATIONAL SINGING, whenever the liturgy is to be celebrated with song: *Episcopi vero ceterique animarum pastores sedulo curent ut in qualibet actione sacra in cantu peragenda universus fidelium coetus actuosam participationem sibi propriam praestare valeat, ad normam art. 28 et 30 (114).*

   AS REPRESENTATIVES OF THE BISHOP, because it is impossible for the bishop always and everywhere to preside over the whole flock in his Church, he cannot do other than establish lesser groups of the faithful. Among these the parishes, set up locally under a pastor who takes the place of the bishop: *Cum Episcopus in Ecclesia sua ipsemet nec semper nec ubique universo gregi praeesse possit, necessario constituere debet coetus, inter quos paroeciae, localiter sub pastore vices gerente Episcopi ordinatae (42).*

TO RESTORE SUNDAY VESPERS, and also the chief hours: *Curent animarum pastores ut Horae praecipuae, praesertim Vesperae, diebus dominicis et festis sollemnioribus, in ecclesia communiter celebrentur (100).*

PENANCE, SACRAMENT OF, rite and formulas to be revised so that they more clearly express both the nature and effect of the sacrament: *Ritus et formulae Paenitentiae ita recognoscantur, ut naturam et effectum Sacramenti clarius exprimant (72).*

PENANCES, ADAPTATION OF LENTEN, to be made in ways that are possible in our own times and in different regions, and according to the circumstances of the faithful: *Paenitentia temporis quadragesimalis . . . Praxis vers paenitentialis, iuxta nostrae aetatis et diversarum regionum possibilitates necnon fidelium condiciones, foveatur (110).*

CHARACTER OF LENTEN, should not only be internal and individual, but also external and social: *Paenitentia temporis quadragesimalis non tantum sit interna et individualis, sed quoque externa et socialis (110).*

WORKS OF, BY MEANS OF, the formation of the faithful is completed in the liturgical year: *Variis denique anni temporibus . . . Ecclesia fidelium eruditionem perficit, per . . . paenitentiae opera (105).*

PENITENTIAL ELEMENTS, LENTEN LITURGY AND, more use to be made, and some which used to flourish in bygone days, are to be restored as may seem good: *elementa baptismalia liturgiae quadragesimalis propria abundantius adhibeantur; quaedam vero ex anteriore tradi-*

tione, pro opportunitate, restituantur; idem dicatur de elementis paenitentialibus (109.a & b).

PIOUS EXERCISES. See DEVOTIONS, POPULAR.

PIOUS PRACTICES, BY MEANS OF, the formation of the faithful is completed in the liturgical year: *Variis denique anni temporibus Ecclesia fidelium eruditionem perficit per pias animi et corporis exercitationes (105).*

POLYPHONY, is admitted into the liturgical celebrations, as long as it accords with the spirit of the liturgical action, as laid down in Art. 30: *Alia genera Musicae sacrae, praesertim vero polyphonia, in celebrandis divinis Officiis minime excluduntur, dummodo spiritui actionis liturgicae respondeant, ad normam art. 30 (116).*

PONTIFICAL, NEW RITE FOR CONCELEBRATION, to be drawn up and inserted: *novus ritus concelebrationis conficiatur, Pontificali . . . inserendus (58).*

  RITE FOR CONSECRATION OF VIRGINS, to be revised: *Ritus Consecrationis Virginum, qui in Pontificali romano habetur recognitioni subiciatur (80).*

  USE, to be restricted to those ecclesiastical persons who have episcopal rank or some particular jurisdiction: *Convenit ut usus pontificalium reservetur illis ecclesiasticis personis, quae aut charactere episcopali, aut peculiari aliqua iurisdictione gaudent (130).*

POPULAR DEVOTIONS. See DEVOTIONS, POPULAR.

PRAYER, BY MEANS OF, the formation of the faithful is completed in the Liturgical year: *variis denique anni temporibus . . . Ecclesia fidelium eruditionem perficit, per . . . precationem (105).*

  PRIVATE, PLACE IN CHRISTIAN LIFE, the Christian indeed is called to pray with his brethren, but he must also enter into his chamber to pray to the Father in secret: *Christianus enim ad communiter orandum vocatus, nihilominus debet etiam intrare in cubiculum suum ut Patrem in abscondito oret (12).*

SECONDARY TO PUBLIC WORSHIP, because every liturgical celebration is an action of Christ the priest and of His body, the Church. No other action of the Church can equal its efficacy by the same title and to the same degree: *Proinde omnis liturgica celebratio, utpote opus Christi sacerdotis, eiusque Corporis, quod est Ecclesia, est actio sacra praecellenter, cuius efficacitatem eodem titulo eodemque gradu nulla alia actio Ecclesiae adaequat (7).*

PRAYER OF THE FAITHFUL, MASS AND, to be restored on Sundays and feasts of obligation, after the gospel and the homily: *"Oratio communis" seu "fidelium" post Evangelium et homiliam, praesertim diebus dominicis et festis de praecepto, restituatur (53).*

> VERNACULAR IN, is permitted: *Linguae vernaculae in Missis cum populo celebratis congruus locus tribui possit, praesertim in . . . "oratione communi" (54).*

PREACHING, CHARACTER OF, is highly esteemed as part of the liturgy itself: *Homilia . . . ut pars ipsius liturgiae valde commendatur (52).*

> CONTENT OF, should be drawn mainly from scriptural and liturgical sources: *haec vero imprimis ex fonte sacrae Scripturae et Liturgiae hauriatur (35.2).*

> OBLIGATION OF, at those Masses which are celebrated with the assistance of the people on Sundays and feasts of obligation, it should not be omitted except for a serious reason: *homilia . . . quinimmo in Missis quae diebus dominicis et festis de praecepto concurrente populo celebrantur, ne omittatur, nisi gravi de causa (52).*

> PURPOSE OF, to expound the mysteries of the faith, and the guiding principles of the Christian life: *homilia . . . fidei mysteria et normae vitae christianae exponuntur (52).*

PRIESTHOOD, UNITY OF, appropriately manifested in concelebration: *concelebratio, qua unitas sacerdotii opportune manifestatur (57:1).*

PRIESTHOOD OF CHRIST, is exercised in the Liturgy: *Merito igitur Liturgia habetur veluti Iesu Christi sacerdotalis muneris exercitatio (7)*.

PRIESTS, INSTRUCTION IN LITURGY, those already working in the Lord's vineyard are to be helped by every suitable means to understand ever more fully what it is that they are doing when they perform the sacred rites: *Sacerdotes, sive saeculares sive religiosi, in vinea Domini iam operantes, omnibus mediis opportunis iuventur ut plenius semper quae in functionibus sacris agunt intellegant (18)*.

   LITURGICAL INNOVATIONS BY, are strictly forbidden: *Quapropter nemo omnino alius, etiamsi sit sacerdos, quidquam proprio marte in Liturgia addat, demat, aut mutet (22:3)*.

   MASS CELEBRATED BY INDIVIDUAL, is still retained as a right, though not at the same time in the same church as a concelebrated Mass, nor on Thursday of the Lord's Supper: *salve tamen semper sit cuique sacerdoti facultas Missam singularem celebrandi, non vero eodem tempore in eadem ecclesia, nec feria V in Cena Domini (57:2.2)*.

   TO GIVE LITURGICAL INSTRUCTIONS, within the rites themselves, at the more suitable moments, and in prescribed or similar words: *Catechesis directius liturgica . . . in ipsis ritibus . . . a sacerdote . . . opportunioribus tantum momentis, praescriptis vel similibus verbis, dicendae, praevideantur (35.3)*.

PRIESTS' CONFERENCES, CONCELEBRATION, is allowed, whether the priests be secular clergy or religious: *facultatem concelebrandi ad sequentes casus Concilio extendere placuit: . . . ad Missas in conventibus cuiusvis generis sacerdotum tum saecularium tum religiosorum (57:1.2.b)*.

PRIME, THE HOUR OF, is suppressed: *Hora Prima supprimatur (89.d)*.

PRIORITY, FEASTS OF THE LORD HAVE, within the entire cycle of the year: *dies festos Domini . . . Proinde Proprium de Tempore aptum suum locum obtineat super festa Sanctorum (108).*

SUNDAY CELEBRATION HAS, and no other celebrations shall have precedence over it unless they be truly of greatest importance: *Itaque dies dominica est primordialis dies festus . . . Aliae celebrationes, nisi revera sint maximi momenti, ipsi ne praeponantur (106).*

PRIVATE PRAYER. See PRAYER.

PROFESSORS, OF LITURGY, in seminaries, religious houses of study, and theological faculties, must be properly trained for their work in institutes which specialize in this subject: *Magistri, qui sacrae Liturgiae disciplinae in seminariis, studiorum domibus religiosis et facultatibus theologicis docendae praeficiuntur, ad munus suum in institutis ad hoc speciali cura destinatis probe instituendi sunt (15).*

OF THEOLOGY, while striving to expound the mystery of Christ and the history of salvation from the angle proper to each of their own subjects, must nevertheless do so in a way which will clearly bring out the connection between their subjects and the liturgy, as also the unity which underlies all priestly training. This applies especially to professors of dogmatic, spiritual, and pastoral theology and to those of holy scripture: *Curent insuper aliarum disciplinarum magistri, imprimis theologiae dogmaticae, sacrae Scripturae, theologiae spiritualis et pastoralis ita, ex intrinsecis exigentiis proprii uniuscuiusque obiecti, mysterium Christi et historiam salutis excolere, ut exinde earum connexio cum Liturgia et unitas sacerdotalis institutionis aperte clarescant (16).*

PSALMODY, BY MEANS OF, active participation is promoted: *Ad actuosam participationem promovendam, populi . . . psalmodia . . . foveantur (30).*

PSALMS, DIVINE OFFICE AND, no longer to be distributed throughout one week, but through some longer period of time: *psalmi non amplius per unam hebdomadam, sed per longius temporis spatium distribuantur (91).*

PSALTER, REVISION OF, already begun, to be finished as soon as possible: *opus recognitionis Psalterii, feliciter inchoatum, quamprimum perducatur ad finem (91).*

PUBLIC WORSHIP. See LITURGY.

RADIO AND TELEVISION, DIRECTOR OF, to be appointed by the bishop: *Transmissiones . . . ope radiophonica et televisifica . . . ductu et sponsione personae idoneae, ad hoc munus ab Episcopo destinatae (20).*

TRANSMISSION OF SACRED RITES, shall be done with discretion and dignity, especially when the service to be broadcast is the Mass: *transmissiones actionum sacrum ope radiophonica et televisifica, praesertim si agatur de Sacro faciendo, discrete ac decore fiant (20).*

READINGS, IN THE MASS, the use of the vernacular is allowed: *Linguae vernaculae in Missis cum populo celebratis congruus locus tribui possit, praesertim in lectionibus (54).*

READINGS OF THE FATHERS, DIVINE OFFICE AND, shall be better selected: *Lectiones de operibus Patrum, Doctorum et Scriptorum ecclesiasticorum depromendae melius seligantur (92.b).*

READINGS OF LIVES OF SAINTS AND MARTYRS, DIVINE OFFICE AND, are to accord with the facts of history: *Passiones seu vitae Sanctorum fidei historiae reddantur (92.c).*

READINGS OF SCRIPTURE, DIVINE OFFICE AND, shall be arranged so that the riches of God's word may be easily accessible in more abundant measure: *Lectio sacrae Scrip-*

turae ita ordinetur, ut thesauri verbi divini in pleniore amplitudine expedite adiri possint (92.a).

LITURGY AND, there is to be more reading in sacred celebrations, and it is to be more varied and suitable: *in celebrationibus sacris abundantior, varior et aptior lectio sacrae Scripturae instauretur (35.1).*

REDEMPTION, MERITS OF, achieved principally by the paschal mystery of Christ's blessed passion, resurrection from the dead, and glorious ascension, whereby "dying, He destroyed our death and, rising He restored our life": *Hoc autem humanae Redemptionis et perfectae Dei glorificationis opus . . . adimplevit Christus Dominus, praecipue per suae beatae Passionis, ab inferis Resurrectionis et gloriosae Ascensionis paschale mysterium, quo "mortem nostram moriendo destruxit, et vitam resurgendo reparavit" (5).*

WORK OF, accomplished in the liturgy: *Liturgia enim, per quam, "opus nostrae Redemptionis exercetur" (2).*

REFORM, LITURGICAL, PURPOSE OF, to impart an ever increasing vigor to the Christian life of the faithful; to adapt more suitably to the needs of our own time those institutions which are subject to change; to foster whatever can promote union among all who believe in Christ; to strengthen whatever can help to call the whole of mankind into the household of the Church: *Sacrosanctum Concilium, cum sibi proponat vitam christianam inter fideles in dies augere; eas institutiones quae mutationibus obnoxiae sunt, ad nostrae aetatis necessitates melius accommodare; quidquid ad unionem omnium in Christum credentium conferre potest, fovere; et quidquid ad omnes in sinum Ecclesiae vocandos conducit, roborare; suum esse arbitratur peculiari ratione etiam instaurandam atque fovendam Liturgiam curare (1).*

REGULARS, ORDERS OF, DIVINE OFFICE AND, who are bound by law or constitution, are obliged to celebrate the entire office in choir: *totum Officium, Ordines . . .*

aliorumque Regularium ex iure vel constitutionibus choro adstrictorum *(95.a)*.

RELICS OF SAINTS, have been traditionally venerated; *Sancti iuxta traditionem in Ecclesia coluntur, eorumque reliquiae authenticae atque imagines in veneratione habentur (111)*.

RELIGIOUS, COMMUNION UNDER BOTH SPECIES AND, may be granted when the bishops think fit: *Communio sub utraque specie . . . tum clericis et religiosis, tum laicis, concedi potest, de iudicio Episcoporum (55)*.

RELIGIOUS IN MAJOR ORDERS, DIVINE OFFICE AND, are bound to recite individually those canonical hours which they do not pray in choir: *Omnes autem illarum Communitatum sodales, qui in Ordinibus maioribus constituti . . . debent eas Horas canonicas soli recitare, quas in choro non persolvunt (95.c)*.

RELIGIOUS IN SOLEMN VOWS, DIVINE OFFICE AND, except lay brothers, are bound to recite individually those canonical hours which they do not pray in choir: *Omnes autem illarum Communitatum sodales, qui sunt . . . solemniter professi, conversis exceptis, debent eas Horas canonicas soli recitare, quas in choro non persolvunt (95.c)*.

RELIGIOUS PROFESSION, CEREMONY OF, should preferably be made within Mass: *professio religiosa laudabiliter intra Missam fiet (80)*.

COMMUNION IN MASS OF, may be granted under both kinds when the bishops think fit: *Communio sub utraque specie . . . concedi potest, de iudicio Episcoporum, veluti . . . professis in Missa religiosae suae professionis (55)*.

RITE OF, shall be drawn up in order to achieve greater unity, sobriety, and dignity. Apart from exceptions in particular law, this rite should be adopted by those who make their profession within the Mass: *Confici-*

atur praeterea ritus professionis religiosae . . . qui ad maiorem unitatem, sobrietatem et dignitatem conferat, ab iis qui professionem intra Missam peragunt, salvo iure particulari assumendus *(80).*

RELIGIOUS SINGING, by the people, is to be skilfully fostered, so that they may contribute their part in devotions, sacred exercises and also during liturgical services: *Cantus popularis religiosus sollerter foveatur, ita ut in piis sacrisque et in ipsis liturgicis actionibus, iuxta normas et praecepta rubricarum, fidelium voces resonare possint (118).*

RENEWAL OF VOWS, rite shall be drawn up in order to achieve greater unity, sobriety, and dignity. Apart from exceptions in particular law, this rite should be adopted by those who make their renewal of vows within Mass: *Conficiatur praeterea ritus . . . renovationis votorum, qui ad maiorem unitatem, sobrietatem et dignitatem conferat, ab iis qui . . . votorum renovationem intra Missam peragunt, salvo iure particulari, assumendus (80).*

RESERVED BLESSINGS, shall be very few; reservations shall be in favor only of bishops or ordinaries: *Benedictiones reservatae perpaucae sint, et in favorem tantum Episcoporum vel Ordinariorum (79).*

RESPONSES, BY MEANS OF, active participation of the people is promoted: *Ad actuosam participationem promovendam, populi . . . responsiones . . . foveantur (30).*

REVERENCES, LITURGY AND, are provided for civil authorities: *In Liturgia . . . praeter honores ad normam legum liturgicarum auctoritatibus civilibus debitos (32).*
apart from those instances defined, they are prohibited to any private person or classes of persons, whether in the ceremonies or by external display: *nulla privatarum personarum aut condicionum, sive in caerimoniis, sive in exterioribus pompis, habeatur acceptio (32).*

ROMAN, the practical norms of the Constitution should be taken as applying only to this rite, except for those which, in the very nature of things, affect other rites as well: *licet normae practicae quae sequunter solum ritum romanum spectare intellegendae sint, nisi agatur de iis quae ex ipsa rei natura alios quoque ritus afficiant (3).*

RITES, ALL LAWFULLY ACKNOWLEDGED, are of equal right and dignity; the Church wishes to preserve them in the future and to foster them in every way: *Sanctam Matrem Ecclesiam declarat omnes ritus legitime agnitos aequo iure atque honore habere, eosque in posterum servari et omnimodo foveri velle (4).*

COMMUNAL FORMS OF, that make provision for a celebration involving the presence and active participation of the faithful, are preferred, as far as possible, to a celebration that is individual and quasi-private: *Quoties ritus, iuxta propriam cuiusque naturam, secum ferunt celebrationem communem, cum frequentia et actuosa participatione fidelium, inculcetur hanc, in* quantum fieri potest, esse praeferendam celebrationi eorundem singulari et quasi privatae (27).

INITIATION, in mission lands, may be adapted to the Christian ritual when possible: *In terris Missionum, praeter ea quae in traditione christiana habentur, illa etiam elementa initiationis admitti liceat . . . quatenus ritui christiano accommodari possunt ad normam art. 37–40 huius Constitutionis (65).*

LATIN, particular law remaining in force, the use of the latin language is to be preserved: *Linguae latinae usus, salvo particulari iure, in Ritibus latinis servetur (36:1).*

NEW FORMS OF, to result in the revision, should be distinguished by a noble simplicity; they should be short, clear, unencumbered by useless repetitions; they should be within the people's powers of comprehension, and normally should not require much explanation: *Exinde in instauratione facienda generales normae quae sequuntur observari debent. Ritus nobili simplicitate fulgeant, sint brevitate perspicui et repetitiones inutiles evitent, sint fidelium captui accommodati, neque generatim multis indigeant explanationibus (34).*

NOTABLE REGIONAL DIFFERENCES, between the rites used in adjacent regions must be carefully avoided: *Caveatur etiam, in quantum fieri potest, ne notabiles differentiae rituum inter finitimas regiones habeantur (23).*

REVISION OF, the Council desires that, where necessary, the rites be revised carefully in the light of sound tradition, and that they be given new vigor to meet the circumstances and needs of modern times: *Concilium . . . optat ut, ubi opus sit, caute ex integro ad mentem sanae traditionis recognoscantur et novo vigore, pro hodiernis adiunctis et necessitatibus, donentur (4).*

SACRAMENTS AND SACRAMENTALS, with the passage of time, certain features have crept in which have rendered their nature and purpose far from clear to the people of today; hence changes have become necessary to adapt them to the needs of our own times: *Cum autem, successu temporum, quaedam in Sacramentorum et Sacramentalium ritus irrepserint, quibus eorum natura et finis nostris temporibus minus eluceant, atque adeo opus sit quaedam in eis ad nostrae aetatis necessitates accommodare (62).*

VERNACULAR IN, may be used according to the norm of Art. 36: *In administratione Sacramentorum et Sacramentalium lingua vernacula adhiberi potest ad normam art. 36 (63.a).*

RITES AND RUBRICS, LITURGICAL BOOKS AND, provisions shall be made for legitimate variations and adaptations to different groups, regions and peoples, especially in mission lands, provided that the substantial unity of the Roman rite is preserved: *servata substantiali unitate ritus romani, legitimis varietatibus et aptationibus ad diversos coetus, regiones, populos, praesertim in Missionibus locus relinquatur, etiam cum libri liturgici recognoscuntur; et hoc in structura rituum et in rubricis instituendis opportune prae oculis habeatur (38).*

RITUALS, NEW SACRAMENTALS, may be added as the need for these becomes apparent: *In Ritualibus recognoscendis ad normam art. 63, etiam nova Sacramentalia, prout necessitas expostulat, addi possunt (79).*

PARTICULAR, shall be prepared in harmony with the new edition of the Roman Ritual, without delay, by the competent territorial ecclesiastical authority mentioned in Art. 22:2 of this Constitution: *Iuxta novam Ritualis romani editionem, Ritualia particularia, a competenti ecclesiastica auctoritate territoriali de qua in art. 22:2 huius Constitutionis quam primum parentur (63.b).*

the instructions prefixed to the individual rites in the Roman Ritual, whether they be pastoral and rubrical, or whether they have special social import, shall not be omitted in drawing up these rituals or particular collections: *In iis autem Ritualibus vel peculiaribus Collectionibus rituum conficiendis, ne omittantur*

instructiones, in Rituali romano singulis ritibus prae-
positae, sive pastoralis et rubricales, sive quae pecu-
liare momentum sociale habent (63.b).

they are to be adapted as regards the language employed, and the needs of the different regions: *singularum regionum necessitatibus, etiam quoad linguam, accommodata (63.b).*

they shall be reviewed by the Apostolic See and then
introduced into the regions for which they have
been prepared: *actis ab Apostolica Sede recognitis,
in regionibus ad quas pertinet adhibeantur (63.b).*

ROMAN MISSAL. *See* MISSAL, ROMAN.

ROMAN PONTIFICAL. *See* PONTIFICAL.

RUBRICS, LITURGICAL BOOKS AND, provisions for the people's parts to be attended to in the revision: *In libris liturgicis recognoscendis, sedulo attendatur ut rubricae
etiam partes fidelium praevideant (31).*

MORE THAN THEIR OBSERVANCE, is required of pastors
when they celebrate the liturgy: *Ideo sacris pastoribus
advigilandum est ut in actione liturgica non solum observentur leges ad validam et licitam celebrationem
(11).*

IN SEMINARIES, clerics must learn how to observe the liturgical laws, so that their life may be thoroughly in-
fluenced by the spirit of the liturgy: *in seminariis . . .
pariter observantiam legum liturgicarum addiscant, ita
ut vita in seminariis et religiosorum institutis liturgico
spiritu penitus informetur (17).*

SACRAMENTALS, ADMINISTRATION, by qualified lay
persons for some, at least in special circumstances and
at the discretion of the ordinary: *Provideatur ut quaedam
Sacramentalia, saltem in specialibus rerum adiunctis et
de iudicio Ordinarii, a laicis congruis qualitatibus praeditis, administrari possint (79).*

INSTITUTION OF, by the Church: *Sacramentalia praeterea sancta Mater Ecclesia instituit (60).*

EFFECTS OF, men are disposed to receive the chief effect of the sacraments, and various occasions in life are rendered holy: *Per ea homines ad praecipuum Sacramentorum effectum suscipiendum disponuntur et varia vitae adiuncta sanctificantur (60).*

NEED FOR CHANGES OF RITES, since, with the passage of time, certain features have crept in which have rendered their nature and purpose far from clear to the people of today: *Cum autem, successu temporum, quaedam in Sacramentorum et Sacramentalium ritus irrepserint, quibus eorum natura et finis nostris temporibus minus eluceant (62).*

NEW KINDS OF, may also be added in the revised rituals as the need for these becomes apparent: *In Ritualibus recognoscendis ad normam art. 63, etiam nova Sacramentalia, prout necessitas expostulat, addi possunt (79).*

RELATED TO SACRAMENTS, they are sacred signs which bear a resemblance to the sacraments: they signify effects, particularly of a spiritual kind, which are obtained through the Church's intercession: *Quae sacra sunt signa quibus, in aliquam Sacramentorum imitationem, effectus praesertim spirituales significantur et ex Ecclesiae impetratione obtinentur (60).*

REVISION OF, to take into account the primary principle of enabling the faithful to participate intelligently, actively and easily; the circumstances of our own days must also be considered: *Sacramentalia recognoscantur, ratione habita normae primariae de conscia, actuosa et facili participatione fidelium, et attentis nostrorum temporum necessitatibus (79).*

SANCTIFYING ACTION OF, well-disposed faithful are given access to the stream of divine grace which flows from the paschal mystery of the passion, death, and resurrection of Christ, the fount from which all sacraments

and sacramentals draw their power: *Itaque liturgia
Sacramentorum et Sacramentalium, id efficit ut fidelibus bene dispositis omnis fere eventus vitae sanctificetur gratia divina manante ex mysterio paschali Passionis, Mortis et Resurrectionis Christi, a quo omnia
Sacramenta et Sacramentalia suam virtutem derivant*
(61).

VERNACULAR, may be used in administering them, according to the norm of Art. 36: *In administratione Sacramentorum . . . Sacramentalium lingua vernacula adhiberi potest ad normam art. 36* (63.a).

SACRAMENTS, CHRIST ABIDES IN, by His power He is
present, so that when a man baptizes, it is really Christ
Himself who baptizes: *Praesens adest virtute sua in Sacramentis, ita ut cum aliquis baptizat, Christus ipse bap-
tizet* (7).

COMMUNAL FORM OF RITES, to be preferred, so far as possible, to a celebration that is individual and quasi-
private: *quoties ritus, iuxta propriam cuiusque naturam, secum ferunt celebrationem communem . . .
in quantum fieri potest esse praeferendam celebrationi
eorundem singulari et quasi privatae* (27).

DIDACTIC ROLE, because they are signs they also instruct:
*Sacramenta . . . ut signa vero etiam ad instructionem
pertinent* (59).

EFFICACY, they do indeed impart grace, but in addition,
the very act of celebrating them most effectively, dis-
poses the faithful to receive this grace in a fruitful
manner, to worship God duly, and to practice charity:
*gratia quidem conferunt, sed eorum celebratio fideles
optime etiam disponit ad eandem gratiam fructuose
recipiendam, ad Deum rite colendum et ad caritatem
exercendam* (59).

EXPRESSION OF FAITH, they not only presuppose faith,
but by words and objects they also nourish, strengthen,
and express it; that is why they are called "sacraments
of faith": *fidem non solum supponunt, sed verbis et*

rebus etiam alunt, roborant, exprimunt; quare fidei
sacramenta dicuntur (59).

NEED FOR CHANGES OF RITES, since, with the passage of
time, certain features have crept in which have rendered their nature and purpose far from clear to the
people of today: *Cum autem, successu temporum,
quaedam in Sacramentorum . . . ritus irrepserint,
quibus eorum natura et finis nostris temporibus minus
eluceant (62).*

NEED TO FREQUENT, with great eagerness since they were
instituted to nourish the Christian life: *Sacramenta
impensissime frequentent, quae ad vitam christianam
alendam sunt instituta (59).*

NEED TO UNDERSTAND SIGNS, is of the greatest importance:
*Maxime proinde interest ut fideles signa Sacramento-
rum facile intellegant (59).*

PURPOSE, to sanctify men, to build up the body of Christ,
and finally, to give worship to God: *Sacramenta ordinantur ad sanctificationem hominum, ad aedificationem Corporis Christi, ad cultum denique Deo reddendum (59).*

SALVIFIC ACTION, for well-disposed members of the faithful they sanctify almost every event in their lives; they
give access to the stream of divine grace which flows
from the paschal mystery of the passion, death, and
resurrection of Christ: *Itaque liturgia Sacramentorum
. . . id efficit ut fidelibus bene dispositis omnis fere
eventus vitae sanctificetur gratia divina manante ex
mysterio paschali Passionis, Mortis et Resurrectionis
Christi (61).*

VERNACULAR, may be used in administering them, according to the norms of Art. 36: *in administratione
Sacramentorum . . . lingua vernacula adhiberi potest
ad normam art. 36 (63.a).*

SACRIFICE, EUCHARISTIC. See MASS.

SAINTS, CULT OF, included in the annual cycle of the Liturgical year: *memorias insuper Martyrum aliorumque*

Sanctorum . . . circulo anni inseruit Ecclesia (104).

FEASTS OF, proclaim the wonderful works of Christ in His servants, and give the faithful fitting examples for their imitation: *Festa Sanctorum mirabilia quidem Christi in servis eius praedicant et fidelibus opportuna praebent exempla imitanda (111). (cf. also 104.)*

RELICS AND IMAGES OF, have been traditionally venerated in the Church: *Sancti iuxta traditionem in Ecclesia coluntur, eorumque reliquiae authenticae atque imagines in veneratione habentur (111).*

RESTRICTION OF FEASTS, to a particular Church or nation or family of religious, is recommended, lest they should take precedence over the feasts of the Mysteries of Christ: *Ne festa Sanctorum festis ipsa mysteria salutis recolentibus praevaleant, plura ex his particulari cuique Ecclesiae vel Nationi vel Religiosae Familiae relinquantur celebranda (111).*

UNIVERSAL FEASTS, only those which are truly of universal importance should be extended to the entire Church: *festa Sanctorum . . . iis tantum ad Ecclesiam universam extensis, quae Sanctos memorant momentum universale revere prae se ferentes (111).*

SANCTIFICATION OF MAN IN THE LITURGY, signified by signs perceptible to the senses, and is effected in a way which corresponds with each of these signs: *Liturgia . . . in qua per signia sensibilia significatur et modo singulis proprio efficitur sanctificatio hominis (7).*

SANCTORAL CYCLE. See YEAR, LITURGICAL.

SATURDAY, HOLY, FAST, where possible to be prolonged throughout the day: *Sacrum tamen esto ieiunium paschale. . . . Sabbato sancto producendum, iuxta opportunitatem (110).*

SCHOLA CANTORUM, to be diligently promoted especially in cathedral churches: *Scholae cantorum assidue provehantur, praesertim apud ecclesias cathedrales (114).*

SCRIPTURE, IMPORTANCE IN THE LITURGY, for it is from scripture that lessons are read and explained in the homily, and psalms are sung; the prayers, collects, and liturgical songs are scriptural in their inspiration, and it is from the scriptures that actions and signs derive their meaning: *Maximum est sacrae Scripturae momentum in Liturgia celebranda. Ex ea enim lectiones leguntur et in homilia explicantur, psalmi canuntur, atque ex eius afflatu instinctuque preces, orationes et carmina liturgica effusa sunt, et ex ea significationem suam actiones et signa accipiunt (24).*

    PRESENCE OF CHRIST IN, since it is He Himself who speaks when the holy scriptures are read in the Church: *Christus praesens adest in verbo suo, siquidem ipse loquitur dum sacrae Scripturae in Ecclesia leguntur (7).*

    PROFESSORS OF, to bring out the connection between their subject and the liturgy: *Curent magistri sacrae Scripturae . . . ut exinde earum connexio cum Liturgia (16).*

    SERMON AND, its content should be drawn mainly from scriptural and liturgical sources: *sermo . . . haec vero imprimis ex fonte sacrae Scripturae et Liturgiae hauriatur (35.2).*

SCRIPTURE READINGS, DIVINE OFFICE AND, shall be rearranged: *lectio sacrae Scripturae ita ordinetur, ut thesauri verbi divini in pleniore amplitudine expedite adiri possint (92.a).*

    LITURGY AND, there is to be more reading in the sacred celebrations, and it is to be more varied and suitable: *In celebrationibus sacris abundantior, varior et aptior lectio sacrae Scripturae instauretur (35.1).*

    MASS AND, a more representative portion will be read to the people in a course of a prescribed number of years: *Quo ditior mensa Verbi Dei paretur fidelibus . . . intra praestitutum annorum spatium, praestantior pars Scripturarum Sanctarum populo legatur (51).*

SCULPTURE, SACRED. *See* STATUES IN CHURCHES.

SEASONS OF THE YEAR, Church infolds the whole mystery of Christ: *Totum vero Christi mysterium per anni circulum explicat, ab Incarnatione et Nativitate usque ad Ascensionem, ad diem Pentecostes et ad expectationem beatae spei et adventus Domini (102).*

ADAPTATIONS, if considered necessary, are to be made in accordance with the provisions of Art. 39 and 40: *Accommodationes autem, secundum locorum condiciones, si quae forte necessariae sint, fiant ad normam art. 39 et 40 (107).*

DISCIPLINE AND CUSTOMS OF, to be preserved or restored to suit the conditions of modern times: *Annus liturgicus ita recognoscatur, ut servatis aut restitutis sacrorum temporum traditis consuetudinibus et disciplinis iuxta nostrae aetatis condiciones (107).*

FORMATION OF FAITHFUL AND, completed by means of pious practices of soul and body, by instruction, prayer, and works of penance: *variis denique anni temporibus iuxta traditas disciplinas, Ecclesia fidelium eruditionem perficit, per pias animi et corporis exercitationes, instructionem, precationem, paenitentiae et misericordiae opera (105).*

HALLOWING GRACE OF THE, recalling thus the mysteries of redemption, the Church opens to the faithful the riches of her Lord's powers and merits, so that these are in some way made present for all time, and the faithful are enabled to lay hold upon them and become filled with saving grace: *Mysteria Redemptionis ita recolens, divitias virtutum atque meritorum Domini sui, adeo ut omni tempore quodammodo praesentia reddantur, fidelibus aperit, qui ea attingant et gratia salutis repleantur (102).*

SEMINARIES, ART APPRECIATION IN, to be fostered so that clerics will be able to appreciate and preserve the Church's venerable monuments, and be in a position to aid, by good advice, artists who are engaged in producing works of art: *Clerici, dum philosophicis et theologicis studiis incumbunt, etiam de Artis sacrae historia eiusque evolutione instituantur, necnon de sanis principiis quibus opera Artis sacrae inniti debent, ita ut Ecclesiae venerabilia monumenta aestiment atque servent, et artificibus in operibus efficiendis congrua consilia queant praebere* (129).

LITURGICAL FORMATION IN, necessary for the spiritual life of clerics: *clerici, in seminariis domibusque religiosis, formationem vitae spiritualis liturgicam acquirant* (17).

PRACTICE OF LITURGICAL LIFE IN, necessary for the liturgical formation of clerics: *Clerici, in seminariis . . . formationem vitae spiritualis liturgicam acquirant* (17).

STUDY OF LITURGY IN, to rank among the compulsory and major courses: *disciplina de sacra Liturgia in seminariis et studiorum domibus religiosis inter disciplinas necessarias et potiores* (16).

in theological faculties, to rank among the principal courses: *in facultatibus autem theologicis inter disciplinas principales est habenda* (16).

to be taught under its theological, historical, spiritual, pastoral, and juridical aspects: *in facultatibus autem theologicis . . . et sub aspectu cum theologico et historico, tum spirituali, pastorali et iuridico tradenda* (16).

TRAINING IN MUSIC IN, is of great importance: *magni habeatur institutio et praxis musica in Seminariis, in Religiosorum utriusque sexus novitiatibus et studiorum domibus* (115).

SEMINARY PROFESSORS, LITURGY AND, to be integrated in the teaching of their own subjects. This consideration is especially important for professors of dogmatic, spiritual, and pastoral theology and sacred scripture: *Curent insuper aliarum disciplinarum magistri, imprimis theologiae dogmaticae, sacrae Scripturae, theologiae spiritualis et pastoralis ita, ex intrinsecis exigentiis proprii uniuscuiusque obiecti . . . ut exinde earum con-nexio cum Liturgia (16).*

SERMON. See PREACHING.

SERVERS, exercise a genuine liturgical function: *minis-trantes . . . vero ministerio funguntur (29).*

> DUTY OF, to discharge their office with sincere piety and decorum: *propterea munus suum tali sincera pietate et ordine exerceant (29).*

> TO BE TRAINED, to perform their functions in a correct and orderly manner: *ad partes suas rite et ordinate obeundas institui (29).*

SEXT, IN CHOIR, to be observed: *In choro, Horae minores . . . Sexta serventur (89.e).*

> OUTSIDE CHOIR, it is lawful to select any one of the three minor hours, according to the respective time of the day: *Extra chorum e tribus unam seligere licet, diei tempori magis congruentem (89.e).*

SHORT OFFICE, CHARACTER OF, recognized as the public prayer of the Church when recited by those who are obliged in virtue of their Constitutions, provided it is drawn up after the pattern of the Divine Office and is duly approved: *Item, publicam Ecclesiae orationem agunt, si quod parvum Officium, vi Constitutionum, recitant, dummodo in modum Officii divini confectum ac rite ap-probatum sit (98).*

SICK, SACRAMENT OF ANOINTING OF. See ANOINTING.

SIGNS, LITURGY AND, the sanctification of man is signified by signs perceptible to the senses, and is effected in a way which corresponds with each of these signs: *liturgia . . . in qua per signa sensibilia significatur et modo sin-gulis proprio efficitur sanctificatio hominis (7).*

> SACRAMENTALS AND, they bear a resemblance to the sacra-ments: they signify effects, particularly of a spiritual kind, which are obtained through the Church's inter-cession: *Sacramentalia . . . quae sacra sunt signa*

sis exceptis, debent eas Horas canonicas soli recitare, quas in choro non persolvunt (95.c).

SONGS, BY MEANS OF, active participation may be promoted: *Ad actuosam participationem promovendam, populi . . . cantica . . . foveantur (30).*

SPECIES, EUCHARISTIC, BOTH FORMS OF, may be granted when the bishops think fit, not only to clerics and religious, but also to the laity, in cases to be determined by the Apostolic See, as, for instance, to the newly ordained in the Mass of their ordination, to the newly professed in the Mass of their profession, and to the newly baptized in the Mass which follows their baptism: *Communio sub utraque specie . . . in casibus ab Apostolica Sede definiendis, tum clericis et religiosis, tum laicis concedi potest, de iudicio Episcoporum, veluti ordinatis in Missa sacrae suae ordinationis, professis in Missa religiosae suae professionis, neophytis in Missa quae Baptismum subsequitur (55).*

SPIRITUAL LIFE, not limited solely to participation in the liturgy: *Vita tamen spiritualis non unius sacrae Liturgiae participatione continetur (12).*

SPIRITUAL THEOLOGY, PROFESSORS OF, to integrate their own subject with the liturgy: *Curent insuper aliarum disciplinarum magistri, imprimis . . . theologiae spiritualis . . . ut exinde earum connexio cum Liturgia aperte clarescant (16).*

SPONSORS, ROLE OF, and also their duties, should be brought out more clearly in the revised rite for the baptism of infants: *ritus baptizandi parvulos recognoscatur . . . partes etiam parentum et patrinorum eorumque officia, in ipso ritu, magis pateant (67).*

STATUES IN CHURCHES, ARRANGEMENT, should reflect right order: *in ecclesiis sacras imagines . . . congruo ordine exponantur (125).*

NUMBER, to be restricted: *attamen moderato numero (125).*

USE OF, to be maintained: *Firma maneat praxis, in ecclesiis sacras imagines fidelium venerationi proponendi
(125).*

SUNDAY, ACTIVE PARTICIPATION IN MASS, is strongly encouraged: *Sacra Synodus vehementer hortatur animarum
pastores ut, catechesi tradenda, fideles sedulo doceant de
integra Missa participanda, praesertim diebus dominicis
et festis de praecepto (56).*

BIBLE SERVICES, should be encouraged especially in places
where no priest is available: *Foveatur sacra Verbi Dei
celebratio . . . in dominicis . . . maxime in locis quae
sacerdote carent (35.4).*

COMMON CELEBRATION OF MASS, to be encouraged within
the parish: *et adlaborandum ut sensus communitatis
paroecialis, imprimis vero in communi celebratione
Missae dominicalis, floreat (42).*

"THE COMMON PRAYER" IN MASS, to be restored, after
the gospel and the homily: *"Oratio communis" seu
"fidelium" post Evangelium et homiliam, praesertim
diebus dominicis restituatur (53).*

PRIMACY OF, over all other celebrations. It shall have
precedence unless other celebrations are truly of greatest importance: *Aliae celebrationes, nisi revera sint
maximi momenti, ipsi ne praeponantur, quippe quae
sit fundamentum et nucleus totius anni liturgici (106).*

REPLACED SABBATH, by a tradition handed down from
the apostles which took its origin from the very day
of Christ's resurrection the Church celebrates the paschal mystery every eighth day: *Mysterium paschale
Ecclesia, ex traditione apostolica quae originem ducit
ab ipsa Resurrectionis Christi, octava quaque die celebrat (106).*

SANCTIFICATION OF, by the faithful gathering together
into one place to take part in the Eucharist, and re-
fraining from labor: *Hac enim die christifideles in
unum convenire debent ut . . . Eucharistiam participantes . . . et vacationis ab opere (106).*

SERMON IN MASS, which is celebrated with the assistance
of the people, may not be omitted except for a serious
reason: *Homilia . . . quinimmo in Missis quae diebus
dominicis . . . concurrente populo celebrantur, ne
omittatur nisi gravi de causa (52).*

VESPERS FOR PEOPLE, to be celebrated in common in
church: *Curent animarum pastores ut Horae praecipuae, praesertim Vesperae, diebus dominicis . . . in
ecclesia communiter celebrentur (100).*

SYNODS, CONCELEBRATION, is permitted: *facultatem concelebrandi . . . ad Missas . . . Synodis (57:1.1.b).*

TABERNACLE, LAWS REGARDING, its position and safety,
to be revised: *canones et statuta ecclesiastica, quae rerum
externarum ad sacrum cultum pertinentium apparatum
spectant, praesertim . . . tabernaculi eucharistici no-
bilitatem, dispositionem et securitatem . . . quam primum recognoscantur (128).*

TELEVISION AND RADIO, DIRECTOR OF, to be appointed by bishop: *Transmissiones actionum sacrarum
ope radiophonica et televisifica . . . ductu et sponsione
personae idoneae, ad hoc munus ab Episcopo destinatae
(20).*

TRANSMISSION OF SACRED RITES AND, to be done with discretion and dignity. This is especially important when
the service to be broadcast is the Mass: *Transmissiones
actionum sacrarum ope radiophonica et televisifica,
praesertim si agatur de Sacro faciendo, discrete ac decore fiant (20).*

TEXTS AND RITES, LITURGY AND, in the restoration they
should be drawn up so that they express more clearly the
holy things which they signify; the Christian people, so
far as possible, should be enabled to understand them
with ease and take part in them fully, actively, and as
befits a community: *Qua quidem instaurationem, textus*

et ritus ita ordinari oportet, ut sancta, quae significant, clarius exprimant, eaque populus christianus, in quantum fieri potest, facile percipere atque plena, actuosa et communitatis propria celebratione participare possit (21).

TEXTS, MUSIC AND, so intended to be sung must always be in conformity with Catholic doctrine; indeed they should be drawn chiefly from holy scripture and from liturgical sources: *Textus cantui sacro destinati catholicae doctrinae sint conformes, immo ex Sacris Scripturis et fontibus liturgicis potissimum hauriantur (121).*

THEOLOGICAL FACULTIES, LITURGY IN, to rank among the principal courses: *in facultatibus autem theologicis inter disciplinas principales est habenda (16).*
  it is to be taught under its theological, historical, spiritual, pastoral, and juridical aspects: *sub aspectu cum theologico et historico, tum spirituali, pastorali et iuridico tradenda (16).*

THEOLOGY, PROFESSORS OF, while striving to expound the mystery of Christ and the history of salvation from the angle proper to each of their own subjects, must nevertheless do so in a way which will clearly bring out the connection between their subject and the liturgy, as also the unity which underlies all priestly training: *Curent insuper aliarum disciplinarum magistri . . . ex intrinsecis exigentiis proprii uniuscuiusque obiecti, mysterium Christi et historiam salutis excolere, ut exinde earum connexio cum Liturgia et unitas sacerdotalis institutionis aperte clarescant (16).*

THURSDAY, HOLY, CONCELEBRATION, is allowed, not only at the Mass of the Chrism, but also at the evening Mass: *facultatem concelebrandi ad sequentes casus Concilio extendere placuit: feria V in Cena Domini tum ad Missam chrismatis, tum ad Missam vespertinam (57:1.1.a).*

TIERCE, IN CHOIR, to be observed: *In choro, Horae Tertia . . . serventur (89.e).*

OUTSIDE CHOIR, it is lawful to select any one of the three minor hours, according to the respective time of the day: *Extra chorum e tribus unam seligere licet, diei tempori magis congruentem (89.e).*

TRANSLATIONS FROM THE LATIN TEXT, into the vernacular intended for use in the Liturgy must be approved by the competent territorial ecclesiastical authority mentioned in Art. 22:2: *Conversio textus latini in linguam vernaculam in Liturgia adhibenda, a competenti auctoritate ecclesiastica territoriali, de qua in art. 22:2, approbari debet (36:4).*

V ATICAN COUNCIL II, AIM OF. See COUNCIL, VATICAN II.

VERNACULAR, BISHOP'S ALLOCUTION IN EPISCOPAL CONSECRATION IN, may be permitted: *Allocutio Episcopi, initio Consecrationis, fieri potest in lingua vernacula (76).*

> IN ORDINATION IN, may be permitted: *Allocutio Episcopi, initio Ordinationis, fieri potest in lingua vernacula (76).*

> COMMON PRAYER IN MASS IN, is permitted: *Linguae vernaculae in Missis cum populo celebratis congruus locus tribui possit, praesertim . . . "oratione communi" (54).*

> DIVINE OFFICE AND, may be granted by the ordinary in individual cases to those clerics for whom the use of the Latin constitutes a grave obstacle to their praying the office properly: *facta tamen Ordinario potestate usum versionis vernaculae ad normam art. 36 confectae concedendi, singulis pro casibus, iis clericis, quibus usus linguae latinae grave impedimentum est quominus Officium debite persolvant (101:1).*

> DIVINE OFFICE FOR NUNS AND NON-CLERICAL INSTITUTES AND, may be granted by the competent superior even in choir, to both men who are not clerics and women. The version, however, must be approved: *Monialiabus,*

necnon sodalibus, sive viris non clericis sive mulieribus, Institutorum statuum perfectionis, in Officio divino, etiam in choro celebrando, concedi potest a Superiore competente ut lingua vernacula utantur, dummodo versio approbata sit (101:2).

LITURGY AND, since the use of the mother tongue, whether in the Mass, administration of the sacraments, or other parts of the liturgy, frequently may be of great advantage to the people, the limits of its employment may be extended: *Cum tamen, sive in Missa, sive in Sacramentorum administratione, sive in aliis Liturgiae partibus, haud raro linguae vernaculae usurpatio valde utilis apud populum exsistere possit, amplior locus ipsi tribui valeat (36:2).*

MORE EXTENDED USE IN MASS, whenever it appears desirable, the regulation laid down in Art. 40 of this Constitution is to be observed: *Sicubi tamen amplior usus linguae vernaculae in Missa opportunus esse videatur, servetur praescriptum art. 40 huius Constitutionis (54).*

NUPTIAL MASS AND, the prayer for the bride may be said in the mother tongue: *Matrimonium ex more intra Missam celebretur . . . oratio super sponsam . . . dici potest lingua vernacula (78).*

PEOPLE'S PARTS AT MASS IN, it is permitted, as local conditions may warrant, according to the norm laid down in Art. 36 of this Constitution: *Linguae vernaculae in Missis . . . ac pro condicione locorum, etiam in partibus quae ad populum spectant, ad normam art. 36 huius Constitutionis (54).*

PRAYERS AND CHANTS IN, is allowed according to regulations laid down separately: *Cum tamen . . . linguae vernaculae usurpatio valde utilis . . . imprimis autem . . . in nonnullis orationibus et cantibus, iuxta normas quae de hac re in sequentibus capitibus singillatim statuuntur (36:2).*

the following provisions are to be observed: for the

Mass, Art. 54; for the sacraments, Art. 63; for the divine office, Art. 101: *Quoad linguam adhibendam, serventur praecepta art. 36; quoad Missam art. 54; quoad Sacramenta, art. 63; quoad Officium divinum, art. 101 (113).*

READINGS AND DIRECTIVES IN, is allowed: *Linguae vernaculae usurpatio valde utilis . . . amplior locus ipsi tribui valeat, imprimis autem in lectionibus et admonitionibus (36:2).*

READINGS AT MASS IN, is allowed: *Linguae vernaculae in Missis cum populo celebratis congruus locus tribui possit, praesertim in lectionibus (54).*

REGULATION OF, is for the competent territorial ecclesiastical authority mentioned in Art. 22:2 to decide whether, and to what extent it is to be used. Their decrees are to be approved, that is confirmed by the Apostolic See. And whenever it seems to be called for, this authority is to consult with bishops of neighboring regions which have the same language: *est competentis auctoritatis ecclesiasticae territorialis, de qua in art. 22:2, etiam, si casus ferat, consilio habito cum Episcopis finitimarum regionum eiusdem linguae, de usu et modo linguae vernaculae statuere, actis ab Apostolica Sede probatis seu confirmatis (36:3).*

VERNACULAR TRANSLATIONS, LITURGY AND, must be approved by the competent territorial ecclesiastical authority mentioned above: *Conversio textus latini in linguam vernaculam in Liturgia adhibenda, a competenti auctoritate ecclesiastica territoriali, de qua supra, approbari debet (36:4).*

VESPERS, CHARACTER OF, an evening prayer: *Vesperae, ut preces vespertinae (89.a).*

SUNDAY, to be restored in parishes: *Curent animarum pastores ut Horae praecipuae, praesertim Vesperae, diebus dominicis et festis sollemnioribus, in ecclesia communiter celebrentur (100).*

VESTMENTS, LAWS REGARDING, to be revised: *Canones et statuta ecclesiastica, quae rerum externarum ad sacrum cultum pertinentium apparatum spectant . . . praesertim quoad . . . decorationis et ornatus rationem (128).*

VIATICUM AND ANOINTING OF THE SICK, CONTINUOUS RITE, shall be drawn up according to which the sick man is anointed after he has made his confession and before he receives viaticum: *Praeter ritus seiunctos Unctionis infirmorum et Viatici, conficiatur Ordo continuus secundum quem Unctio aegroto conferatur post confessionem et ante receptionem Viatici (74).*

VIGILS, BIBLE SERVICES AND, should be encouraged, especially on the vigils of the more solemn feasts: *Foveatur sacra Verbi Dei celebratio in solemniorum festorum pervigiliis (35.4).*

WATER, BAPTISMAL, except during Eastertide, it may be blessed within the rite of baptism itself by an approved shorter formula: *Aqua baptismalis, extra tempus paschale, in ipso ritu Baptismi probata formula breviore benedici potest (70).*

WEDDING, CEREMONY OF, is normally to be celebrated within the Mass, after the reading of the gospel and the homily, and before "the prayer of the faithful": *Matrimonium ex more intra Missam celebretur, post lectionem Evangelii et homiliam, ante "orationem fidelium" (78).*

OUTSIDE MASS, the epistle and gospel from the nuptial Mass are to be read at the beginning of the rite, and the blessing should always be given to the spouses: *Si vero Sacramentum Matrimonii sine Missa celebratur, Epistola et Evangelium Missae pro sponsis legantur in initio ritus et benedictio sponsis semper impertiatur (78).*

WORLD, INTERCESSION ON BEHALF OF, provided for in "the common prayer" to be restored in the Mass on Sun-

days and feasts of obligation: "*Oratio communis*" *seu*
"*fidelium*" . . . *praesertim diebus dominicis et festis de
praecepto, restituatur . . . obsecrationes fiant . . . totiusque mundi salute (53).*

WORSHIP, OF CHURCH, is liturgy which is performed by
the mystical body of Jesus Christ, that is, by the Head
and His members: *a mystico Iesu Christi Corpore, Capite nempe eiusque membris, integer cultus publicus
exercetur (7).*

> REGULATION OF, depends solely on the authority of the
> Church, that is, on the Apostolic See, and as laws may
> determine, on the bishop: *Sacrae Liturgiae moderatio
> ab Ecclesiae auctoritate unice pendet: quae quidem est
> apud Apostolicam Sedem et, ad normam iuris, apud
> Episcopum (22:1).*

> in virtue of power conceded by the law, within certain
> defined limits it belongs also to the various kinds of
> competent territorial bodies of bishops legitimately
> established: *Ex potestate a iure concessa, rei litur-
> gicae moderatio inter limites statutos pertinet quo-
> que ad competentes varii generis territoriales Epis-
> coporum coetus legitime constitutos (22:2).*

YEAR, LITURGICAL, ADAPTATIONS, if considered necessary
on account of local conditions, are to be made in accordance with the provisions of Art. 39 and 40: *annus liturgicus . . . accommodationes autem, secundum locorum
condiciones, si quae forte necessariae sint, fiant ad normam art. 39 et 40 (107).*

> EASTER AND, the Council would not object if it were as-
> signed to a particular Sunday of the Gregorian Calen-
> dar, provided that those to whom it may concern, espe-
> cially the brethren who are not in communion with the
> Apostolic See, give their assent: *Sacrosanctum Con-
> cilium non obnititur quin festum Paschatis certae do-*

minicae *in Calendario Gregoriano assignetur, assentientibus iis quorum intersit, praesertim fratribus ab
Apostolicae Sedis communione seiunctis (Appendix 1).*

FEASTS OF BLESSED VIRGIN IN, occupy a prominent place
in the annual cycle of Christ's mysteries: *in hoc annuo
mysteriorum Christi circulo celebrando, Sancta Ecclesia Beatam Mariam Dei Genetricem cum peculiari
amore veneratur (103).*

FEASTS OF THE LORD IN, the minds of the faithful must
be directed primarily toward these. Therefore, the
proper of the time shall be given the preference which
is its due over the feasts of the saints: *Fidelium animi
dirigantur imprimis ad dies festos Domini . . . proinde Proprium de Tempore aptum suum locum obtineat super festa Sanctorum (108).*

FEASTS OF THE SAINTS IN, occupy a place of honor:
*Memorias insuper Martyrum aliorumque Sanctorum
. . . circulo anni inseruit Ecclesia (104).*

only those of truly universal importance should be extended to the universal Church: *iis tantum ad Ecclesiam universam extensis, quae Sanctos memorant
momentum universale revera prae se ferentes (111).*

to be restricted to a particular Church or nation or
family of religious, lest they should take precedence
over the feasts which commemorate the very mysteries of salvation: *Ne festa Sanctorum festis ipsa
mysteria salutis recolentibus praevaleant, plura ex
his particulari cuique Ecclesiae vel Nationi vel Religiosae Familiae relinquantur celebranda (111).*

SERMONS DURING, to expound the mysteries of faith and
the guiding principles of the Christian life: *Homilia,
qua per anni liturgici cursum ex textu sacro fidei mysteria et normae vitae christianae exponuntur (52).*

TO BE REVISED, so that the traditional customs and discipline of the sacred seasons shall be preserved or restored
to suit the conditions of modern times: *Annus liturgicus ita recognoscatur ut, servatis aut restitutis sacro-*

rum temporum traditis consuetudinibus et disciplinis
iuxta nostrae aetatis condiciones (107).

SUNDAY IN, is truly of greatest importance. Other celebrations shall not have precedence over it unless they
be truly of greatest importance: dies dominica . . .
aliae celebrationes, nisi revera sint maximi momenti,
ipsi ne praeponantur, quippe quae sit fundamentum et
nucleus totius anni liturgici (106).

VARIOUS SEASONS OF, are hallowed by pious practices for
soul and body, by instruction, prayer, and works of
penance and of mercy: Variis denique anni temporibus
iuxta traditas disciplinas Ecclesia fidelium eruditionem
perficit, per pias animi et corporis exercitationes, instructionem, precationem, paenitentiae et misericordiae
opera (105).